MARIANO FORTUNY: HIS LIFE AND WORK

GUILLERMO DE OSMA

AURUM PRESS

TEXT © GUILLERMO DE OSMA 1980
© AURUM PRESS LTD. 1980
PUBLISHED BY AURUM PRESS LIMITED, 11 GARRICK STREET,
LONDON W.C.2.

FIRST PRINTING

ISBN 0 906053 11 0

DESIGNED BY TERRY JONES AND NEIL H. CLITHEROE
PRINTED IN HOLLAND BY L. VAN LEER & COMPANY LIMITED

A MIS PADRES

CONTENTS

Acknowledgements

Although, like any other work of its type, this book is technically the work of a single person, it would never have achieved its goal without the co-operation, advice, interest and enthusiasm of numerous people. First and foremost I should like to thank Countess Gozzi, without whom this book could never have been written. She knew Mariano Fortuny personally from an early age and worked with him until his death. Even today she continues to supervise the smooth running of Fortuny, Inc., carrying on the production of those superb printed cottons that Fortuny himself first introduced and which, thanks to her tireless efforts, are now famous throughout the world. Her love for Mariano's work has led her to seek out and preserve any item connected with him, whether it be a passing reference in some small provincial newspaper or one of his marvellous dresses. This material, combined with her first-hand knowledge of both the artist and his work, all of which she placed at my disposal, has been fundamental to my understanding of Fortuny's life.

I should also like to thank my publishers: Tim Chadwick, who believed in Fortuny, in me and in my book, even before I had started the actual business of writing it; and Michael Haggiag, who has worked tirelessly at converting what was initially a somewhat over-academic text into something eminently readable. I am further indebted to Terry Jones and Neil Clitheroe for the skill and imagination with which they designed these pages, and to Ray Martin and Angela Dyer for invaluable editorial assistance.

In preparing this book I have made the acquaintance of a number of marvellous people, notably Cecilia and Mariano de Madrazo, Fortuny's first cousins. I shall not forget the time I spent in Venice in the company of Cecilia, a remarkably kind, lovely and wise lady. Mariano, too, was of invaluable help to me. From our first meeting, this great man, who I am now proud to call a friend, placed his knowledge and experience, his archives and his collection entirely at my disposal.

My thanks also go to my friend Eduardo Momeñe, a fine photographer, who travelled to Venice at his own expense and within the space of a few days took photographs of a vast quantity of objects that interested me. He also acted as a continual source of inspiration and encouragement throughout this work. In addition, I owe a great deal to my professors Julián Gallego and Alfonso Perez Sanchez, vice-director of the Museo del Prado, both of whom gave me considerable advice and help. I am also grateful to the staff of the Musée Historique des Tissus in Lyons, especially Evelyn Gaudry, Jean Michel Tuchscherer, Marie Dominique Frieh, Gabriel Vial and Odile Valansot.

I received invaluable assistance from a number of collectors and dealers, who allowed me to study, photograph and admire their dresses and materials: notably Liselotte Höhs, who gave me such a warm welcome when I visited her marvellous collection in Venice; and Tina Chow, who repeatedly granted my requests to see her collection and was even prepared to model her dresses for Eduardo to photograph; also C. Z. Guest, Philippa Franses, Veru and Roland Shamask and Mark Walsh. I would also like to thank Lauren Hutton for the photographs she allowed us to take of her in Fortuny's dresses.

Working in American museums was a delight and the people there helped me in every way possible. I should particularly like to mention Stella Blum and Diana Vreeland from the Metropolitan Museum in New York and Ann Coleman from the Brooklyn Museum. The staff of the Victoria and Albert Museum in London were also very helpful, particularly Valerie Mendes, the assistant keeper of twentieth-century fashion.

My thanks must also go to Geoffrey Culverwell for his translation from the Spanish and to my friends in the Calcografía Nacional in Madrid, as well as to Bianca Cavaglieri, who was such a perfect hostess in Venice; to Ana Figueras, who typed part of the manuscript without charge; to the Marqués de Santofloro; and many of my friends, who took a great interest in my work and continually encouraged it. To all these people and many others I owe the ultimate success of this book.

Foreword

When I first met Mariano Fortuny I immediately felt myself in the presence of a creative genius and a rare human being. I also knew that my future would involve a close collaboration with him. The most generous of mentors, he enjoyed exchanging ideas with me, and it was tacitly accepted that I would eventually be privileged to carry on his work. After his death in 1949 I responded to the challenge by taking over his textile factory on the Giudecca in Venice and kept his name and work alive there as well as through my other organization, Fortuny, Inc. of New York. Through the years I have always been guided by his strict standards of artistic excellence.

Often described as a latter-day 'Renaissance man', Fortuny was essentially an innovator and an original. He worked in many fields and influenced numerous artists and designers. There have even been direct attempts to copy his creations, particularly the gowns and the textiles. As a result the truth has occasionally been distorted, and myths and fallacies have arisen about both artist and man.

Over many years I have longed for the opportunity to set the record straight, and that chance has now arisen through the painstaking research of Mr Guillermo de Osma. I have given him the benefit of my personal recollections and allowed him free access to the large collection of documents, photographs and other material in my personal archives. The outcome is the present book, which I sincerely hope will be a pleasure and an inspiration to all its readers.

ELSIE LEE GOZZI

Giudecca, Venice

THE FAMILY TREE

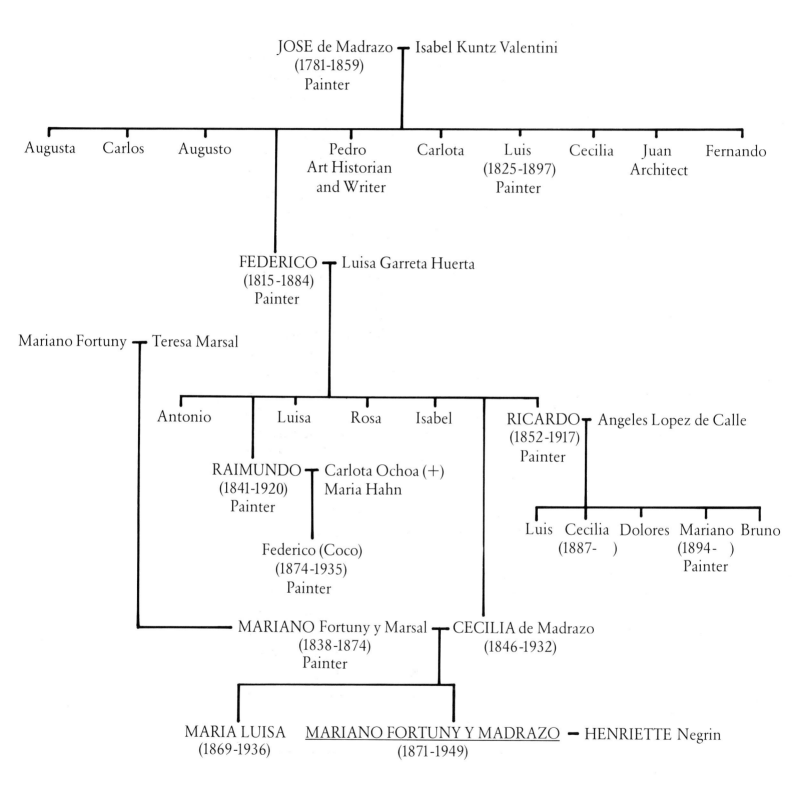

JOSE de Madrazo — Isabel Kuntz Valentini
(1781-1859)
Painter

Augusta   Carlos   Augusto   Pedro   Carlota   Luis   Cecilia   Juan   Fernando
                                 Art Historian   (1825-1897)   Architect
                                 and Writer   Painter

FEDERICO — Luisa Garreta Huerta
(1815-1884)
Painter

Mariano Fortuny — Teresa Marsal

Antonio   Luisa   Rosa   Isabel   RICARDO — Angeles Lopez de Calle
                                              (1852-1917)
                                              Painter

RAIMUNDO — Carlota Ochoa (+)
(1841-1920)   Maria Hahn
Painter

Luis   Cecilia   Dolores   Mariano   Bruno
        (1887-)   (1894-)
                               Painter

Federico (Coco)
(1874-1935)
Painter

MARIANO Fortuny y Marsal — CECILIA de Madrazo
(1838-1874)   (1846-1932)
Painter

MARIA LUISA   MARIANO FORTUNY Y MADRAZO — HENRIETTE Negrin
(1869-1936)   (1871-1949)

Preface

This book is the first attempt, as far as I know, to provide a methodical account of Mariano Fortuny's life and work. It is based on all the evidence, written and verbal, that it was possible for me to assemble. Yet the story is also far from complete. Even during his life, Fortuny was regarded as something of an enigma, and undoubtedly many secrets died with him. The essays and articles that have been written about him are almost always brief and superficial. He is spoken of as a magician, an alchemist, a dreamer, a Renaissance man, an original genius, etc., but there is never any real attempt to justify these descriptions. The aura of mystery and poetry that was to surround him throughout his life, his strange family background, the highly personal way that his work developed on the fringe of contemporary artistic movements, the fantastic Palazzo Orfei, the theatrical quality of all his work, his relationships, the sophisticated world of his admirers and the varied and apparently unconnected nature of the fields in which he worked, all combined to make it both tempting and easy, much too easy, to indulge in mythologizing and literary fantasizing. Of course Fortuny *was* a magician, but there are two types of magician and two types of magic: Merlin and his spells, and the artist and his creative abilities. It is, I hope, the latter kind of magic to which I always refer. Each may achieve a similar result: a mysterious transformation of reality and the people who come into contact with that reality. Yet Merlin has only to say 'abracadabra', whereas the artist has to proceed down a long and sometimes tortuous road to achieve the same effect. Because of this difference, the first is purely mythical, while the second is of the stuff from which myths are made. I do not think it is necessary to perpetuate the myths about Fortuny – his 'reality' is fascinating enough – and have attempted to deal with his life and work as fairly and objectively as possible, if indeed it is possible to deal critically with a personality who constantly eludes classifications and definitions. This book should be regarded as an attempt to do justice to a man who was not only a creator of works of art, but also of a whole personal world. This was his greatest achievement: the creation of a Baroque world, built of fantasy and reality, of science and magic, of art and of life. In order to understand and penetrate it one must first accept that it was created by and for the artist himself. It contained only one principle and one rule: Mariano Fortuny. He was both its protagonist and its *raison d'être*.

GUILLERMO DE OSMA

THE FORMATIVE YEARS

One must not seek to be modern simply by doing what hasn't been done before, for this leads to extravagance; on the contrary one should co-ordinate the efforts of the preceding ages to show how our century can best accept its heritage and make use of it.

GUSTAVE MOREAU

Mariano Fortuny created some of the most remarkable fabrics and dresses of this century. His pleated silk gowns and velvet cloaks are regarded by collectors and museums around the world as the unique expression and embodiment of a craft at its best. Yet he was hardly a *couturier* in the usual sense of the term. A painter by training, he adapted the line of his dresses to the natural shape of a woman's body and sought to develop a type of garment that would not be subject to the whims of fashion. Indeed, he was vigorously opposed to the restrictive and unnatural fashions of his time, and remained aloof from the commercial world which produced them.

A man of far-reaching interests, Fortuny was as well versed in physics and chemistry as he was in the arts. His dresses and textiles, while certainly his most enduring achievements, represent only one aspect of a rich, creative output. Between 1901 and 1934 he registered more than twenty inventions in Paris, ranging from a system for varying the intensity of arc lamps to a means of propelling boats. He also obtained patents for the design of his most famous gown, the Delphos, as well as a series of new textile-printing processes and a revolutionary system of stage lighting. None of his activities can be understood in isolation, however, or appreciated in any significant way except as an integral part of the artist's whole life and work.

Mariano Fortuny y Madrazo was born in Granada, the ancient Moorish capital of Spain, in 1871. His name derived, in the Spanish fashion, from a linking of the first surnames of his father and mother. Both sides of his family included well-known artists who were to have a strong influence on

Portrait of Mariano c. 1880. Fortuny spent his childhood and early youth in Paris where this delicate watercolour was painted by his uncle Ricardo de Madrazo. (Mariano de Madrazo, Spain)

Portrait of Mariano's mother, Cecilia Fortuny, c. 1882/3 by Antonio Boldini, a fashionable portraitist of the period and admirer of her late husband, Mariano Fortuny y Marsal. (Mariano de Madrazo, Spain/Archivo Mas)

Right: Portrait of Mariano Fortuny y Marsal by his father-in-law, Federico de Madrazo, the most famous Spanish portraitist of his time and for many years director of the Prado Museum in Madrid. (Museo de Arte Moderno, Barcelona/Archivo Mas)

his development, imbuing him with a sense of tradition and history, and giving him a taste for the cultural achievements of the past.

His father, Mariano Fortuny y Marsal, was a painter who by the age of thirty-three already enjoyed an international reputation, and spent his life travelling between Italy, Spain and France. His paintings on Arab subjects, his nostalgic recreations of eighteenth-century court life, and his luminous landscapes delighted art critics and collectors alike. The critic Theophile Gautier wrote of him that 'as an etcher he is the equal of Goya and close to Rembrandt',[1] while the painter Henri Regnault exclaimed in a letter to a friend: 'He is master to us all. If you could only see the two or three pictures he's completing at the moment and the watercolours that he's done recently. It makes me feel disgusted with my own . . . oh Fortuny, you give me sleepless nights!'[2]

In 1866 he married Cecilia de Madrazo, who herself belonged to a prominent family of Spanish painters, architects and critics. Her grandfather, José de Madrazo, had been responsible for introducing Neo-classicism into Spain, while her father, Federico de Madrazo, was court painter to Queen Isabel II as well as director of the already famous Prado Museum in Madrid. At first the couple divided their time between Rome, where the artist kept a studio, and Paris, where his agent Goupil was selling his work for fabulous prices. In 1870, however, with the outbreak of the Franco-Prussian War, they abandoned Paris for Spain, passing through Madrid and Seville before settling in Granada with their one-year-old daughter María Luisa. Mariano was born the following year, but the family only stayed in the city until the end of 1872 when another war, the Third Carlist War, forced them to return to Rome.

The elder Fortuny had a passion for collecting *objets d'art*. In the towns of southern Spain, in the villages of North Africa, in the antique markets of the European capitals, he sought out rare pieces of Hispano-Moresque pottery, Persian carpets, Islamic metalwork and armoury of every sort, all of which accumulated in his Roman villa alongside antique Spanish furniture and a rich collection of traditional fabrics and textiles. The young Mariano grew up amidst this profusion of treasures. As a child they aroused his curiosity; later they inspired many of his own motifs, ideas and constructions.

During the summer of 1874, Fortuny y Marsal contracted malaria while on holiday with his family on the outskirts of Naples. He died in Rome the following November at the age of thirty-six and at the height of his brilliant career. Mariano was then only three years old, but the figure of

his father left an indelible mark on his work and personality. He idolized him and was forever seeking ways to keep his memory alive.

Having inherited a fine collection of his paintings, drawings and watercolours, Mariano was not content to preserve and copy them, but also added to them. He personally printed a number of his father's etchings, the plates of which he guarded carefully, as well as making extensive studies of his works and keeping in touch with museums and collectors in order to provide them with any information they might need. He wrote a letter of congratulations to the Board of the Museos de Barcelona when they acquired *La Vicaria* in 1922, the elder Fortuny's most famous painting, and it is interesting to note that similar congratulations were sent from Paris by José Maria Sert and Pablo Picasso. In 1933 he edited a handsome book on his father for a Milanese publisher, entitled *Mariano Fortuny 1838–1874*, copies of which he bound himself using his own fabrics. Mariano also preserved hundreds of objects that had been in his father's collections, including such personal memorabilia as his palette and worktable, both of which he always kept by his side.

View of the courtyard of the Alhambra in Granada, the ancient capital of Moorish Spain and city of Mariano's birth.

The link between father and son consisted of more than a hallowed memory. Both of them were great travellers, and both were fascinated by the Arab world and by the exotic; they collected the same kind of objects and their places of work were remarkably similar. Yet this similarity resulted less from the objects themselves than from the way they were arranged and displayed. Both men liked to use textiles as the main decorative medium; they shared a taste for models wearing tunics or draped with lengths of material, and for hanging tapestries or textiles from the ceiling in order to break up the vast spaces of their studios. Like his father, who designed his own armour and was fascinated by the technical skills of the craftsman,[3] Mariano had a passionate curiosity for the way things worked and took an early interest in mechanics and technical problems. If the elder Fortuny anticipated many of his son's talents, it was the latter who gave full expression to the embryonic capacities for design and invention in the father.

After the death of her husband, Doña Cecilia took her two children Mariano and María Luisa to Paris where her brother Raymundo had become a celebrated portrait painter of the *Belle Epoque* society. There she organized a small salon for the friends and followers of her late husband and, eager for her son to follow in his father's footsteps, encouraged him to start painting under the guidance of his uncle when he was only seven years old. Through his family Mariano came to know many of the artists of his father's generation, men such as Benjamin Constant, Paul Baudry and Jean Louis Meis-

Left: The Fortuny family in the garden of their Roman villa, c. 1872. Doña Cecilia, holding a parasol, is seated in the foreground with Mariano and his sister, María Luisa. Her husband is standing behind them on the steps. (Mariano de Madrazo, Spain)

The Fortunys surrounded by friends and relatives in Rome c. 1872. The villa was a meeting place for artists, critics and collectors for whom Fortuny y Marsal was one of the greatest living painters. Mariano is being held in the arms of an aunt. (Mariano de Madrazo, Spain)

sonier, who represented the academic style of painting, which was already under attack from the Realists, Impressionists and Symbolists who were opening the way to modern art. The young Fortuny was certain to have attended the exhibitions of the *avant garde* painters, but he soon lost interest in the polemics which surrounded their art, preferring instead to listen to his uncles, his grandfather and their friends speak of their more traditional approach to painting and the great masters of the past. Throughout his life he would copy paintings by Tiepolo, Rubens, Velazquez, Carpaccio, Titian and Tintoretto, with the intention of learning every detail of their technique. As a result he became an expert restorer and in later life assisted several important restoration projects in his adopted city of Venice.

As well as painting, Mariano also learned etching at an early age and constantly transcribed the same scenes from one medium into another. His work as a painter and an etcher was extensive and varied. He made portraits of his mother, his sister, his friends, as well as a number of society ladies. There were also numerous self-portraits which attested to a certain amount of self-preoccupation and introspection. Other subjects include landscapes of Venice, Rome, Granada, Vicenza, Morocco and Egypt; still-lifes of

Fortuny's father died before he could complete this rare portrait of his children, seen playing in the Japanese room of their Roman villa. Maria Luisa is amusing herself with a fan, while Mariano is entangled in a piece of material. 1874. (Museo del Prado, Madrid)

nature; floral compositions inspired by works of his father; and subjects taken from old masters such as Tiepolo, Rembrandt or Michelangelo. He painted whatever interested him in a style which did not correspond to any particular school or artistic grouping and which reflected preoccupations of colour and form associated with the art of the past. His pictorial output, while undoubtedly the most flawed aspect of his work, provides the key to his other activities. Through painting, he learned the subtle uses and harmonies of colour. His fabrics were themselves conceived as paintings: dyed in successive layers of colours to create special interplays of light, printed and retouched by hand with the aid of a paintbrush and other instruments, each roll possessed unique textures and patterns that were never repeated.

Mariano suffered from an allergy to horses which provoked frequent attacks of asthma and hay fever throughout his early life. In 1889, therefore, his mother, who in any case thought Paris had become too expensive and noisy, decided to move again, this time to Venice. A silent, melancholy city devoid of horses and carriages and living in the memory of its glorious past, it seemed to mirror her state of mind and provide the ideal solution to her

Fortuny y Marsal with his brothers-in-law Ricardo (far left) and Raymundo (far right) de Madrazo, both of whom were painters. The Madrazos were a prominent family of Spanish artists and critics who had a strong influence on Mariano's artistic development. (Mariano de Madrazo, Spain)

problems. In addition it had a powerful sentimental appeal since her husband, who only became familiar with the city in the last year of his life, had expressed a great desire to return there and paint in the Venetian light which had so intrigued him. In her new residence on the Grand Canal, the stately Palazzo Martinengo in San Gregorio, Doña Cecilia had room to hang her husband's many paintings, display his vast collection of *objets d'art*, and recreate an atmosphere in which his presence was strongly felt.

Coco de Madrazo by his father, Raymundo, a famous portraitist of the Belle Epoque. *A cousin and childhood companion of Mariano, Coco became a prominent figure in Parisian society and helped to promote his work. (Mariano de Madrazo, Spain)*

For the eighteen-year-old Mariano, life in this timeless Venice, this nostalgic souvenir of history that still recalled the flavour of the East, reinforced his conviction that the study of the past would teach him more than if he immersed himself in the current confusion of artistic styles and doctrines. In the evening he attended a drawing class to refine his technique, but during the day he visited the art galleries and churches, studied ancient treatises on painting, and explored the streets, piazzas and canals with his paint brushes and camera in hand. Photography, a new development which Fortuny greatly admired, became for him an experimental tool and an adjunct to his painting. Like many other painters of the period he used it to make preliminary studies for many of his canvases. Ironically his photographs, like his etchings, have a power and vitality of their own which often surpass that of his paintings.

In 1892 Mariano, having been introduced to Wagner's work in Paris, decided to visit Bayreuth, where the composer had built a theatre especially designed for his operas with the help of Ludwig II of Bavaria, the 'dream king'. There Fortuny fell under the spell of the German composer, returning to Venice with his outlook on art totally transformed. For the next few years he dedicated himself almost exclusively to illustrating Wagnerian themes. It was not simply the world of images inspired by Wagnerian legends which attracted Mariano, however, but something much more important. For Wagner, art had an obligation to purify and transform, and this mission could not be accomplished with any effect unless art was thought of as a superior phenomenon. Art in the total sense was an integration of all the artistic disciplines: an integration which found its epitome in the Wagnerian musical drama where poetry, painting, music, song, dance and architecture all had an equal place.

A new way of looking at art had also been proposed by the movement for reform in the applied arts which originated in England in the mid nineteenth century and later developed into the Aesthetic Movement and finally into Art Nouveau. Although the leaders of this movement – Morris, Crane, Mackintosh, Van de Velde – approached art from a very different perspective to Wagner, they also rejected the hierarchies and barriers between the arts, proposing a new order in which designer and craftsman would work together as one, and in which the goal was not only the end product but the total process from the original idea to its ultimate realization. For William Morris, the quality of an object could only be improved by an intimate knowledge of its raw materials and the different stages in its production, and to this end he prepared the pigments for his paintings, wove his own textiles, and produced books for which he made the ink, the plates, and even the typographic moulds.

In the solitude and independence of his Venetian studio Fortuny, while closer in spirit to Wagner than to Morris, nonetheless arrived at the same conclusion as the latter: paintings, etchings, photographs, fabrics and clothing, all had equal value as works of art. The artist had to control every step of the creative process, or better still, know how to make everything himself.

Mariano's insatiable curiosity led him to pursue an astonishing range of disciplines. Already painter, etcher, sculptor and photographer, he became a lighting engineer, an inventor, a theatre director, a set designer, an architect and finally a creator of exquisite fabrics and clothes. Everything seemed to be a source of fascination for him and he launched himself into all kinds of research with boundless energy and enthusiasm. He manufactured his own dyes and pigments according to the ancient methods of early masters, pulled his own etchings on the great hand-press in his library, invented his own photographic paper for developing prints, designed lamps and furniture for his home, constructed model theatres and stage sets, designed the machinery for printing his materials, made dresses and even bound his own books.

The start of Fortuny's most creative period coincided with his move to the Palazzo Pesaro Orfei in 1899. A magnificent palace built in the thirteenth century for the Pesaro family, it was an ideal work place, a building full of large open spaces in which he could give full rein to his various talents. Here he could control not only the whole creative process, but also the world in which that process took place. The Palazzo Orfei eventually became the Palazzo Fortuny, the 'house of the magician'. One journalist wrote: 'Last night I entered the mysterious *palazzo* and was spellbound by his magic: I passed in front of lamps as bright as suns and my body threw no shadow; I saw, spread out on the walls of the immense rooms or enclosed in dazzling glass cases, many-coloured hangings, brocades and damasks of which not a thread was woven. I passed into a

remote, shut-up room and saw the sky, a real sky, in calm and stormy weather, extending all round a vast amphitheatre.'[4]

The *palazzo* had two entrances, one through the quiet Campo di S. Benedetto, the other through a narrow alleyway which led into a courtyard. At the top of the stairs was the *piano nobile*, which except for a few adjoining sitting rooms was taken up almost entirely by Fortuny's great salon-studio, one of the largest covered areas in Venice. While he and his wife Henriette received friends there and entertained, it was basically a room dedicated to work, where Mariano liked to paint bathed in the magical light that filtered through the thick Venetian glass of the enormous windows. There hung his textiles, alongside those he had inherited from his father: vast lengths of velvet that covered the walls and divided the great room like enormous curtains. On these materials were placed his paintings and those of his father, interspersed with arms and armour, and glass display cabinets, chests and other pieces of furniture in which were stored or exhibited religious vestments, his own velvet capes, pieces of sculpture, Gemito's bust of his father, together with one of himself as a child and ones of his uncles, more arms and other curiosities such as the funerary masks of

La Vicaria *(The* Vicarage*), 1868–70, was Fortuny y Marsal's most famous painting. Purchased by the Parisian art dealer Goupil, it received wide acclaim when first exhibited in his gallery at the Place de l'Opera. The gentleman holding a sabre is the painter Meissonier. (Museo de Arte Moderno, Barcelona/ Archivo Mas)*

Beethoven and Wagner. From the ceiling there hung lamps of his own design, trapezoidal, conical or elliptical, made from silk painted with geometrical patterns, looking somewhat oriental. When the walls were not covered in fabrics and *objets d'art*, they were painted with frescoes done by Fortuny himself in a strange style somewhere between the conventional and the Mannerist.

The library above the *piano nobile* was his 'holy of holies', containing not only his books, many of them bound by Henriette using his materials, but also his engraving tools and his 'alchemist's' equipment. It was there that he etched his copper plates, and printed them on his own manual press; there that he prepared his pigments, the tempera colours whose secrets he had learned from old craftsmen, heirs to a medieval tradition that still survived in parts of Italy. It was also in the library that Fortuny prepared, to precise formulas, the dyes with which he laboriously worked, layer upon layer, to achieve the mysteriously changing and transparent colour of his velvets. These in turn were produced in workshops on the top floor of the *palazzo*.

For his experiments, however, Fortuny had to leave the library, since there was not enough room for his models and theatrical maquettes, some of which occupied the sitting rooms off the main salon-studio. Here he kept the early models of his dome for indirect lighting, complete with reduced-scale lights, spotlights and scenery.

Other projects were taking shape on the top floor, where 'in an attic beneath the eaves, by means of a projector he conjured up at dead of night the gigantic head of one of Michelangelo's Sibyls or a storm-tossed landscape by Leonardo.'[5]

In spite of the grandiose and exotic atmosphere of Palazzo Orfei, its inhabitants led a fairly austere working life. The private rooms, situated in a tower attached to the side of the courtyard entrance, were small and monastic. Henriette made the beds herself and took care of her husband's clothes: his cousin Mariano de Madrazo recalls how Henriette used to wash and iron the white cravat that he usually wore.

Fortuny was about six feet tall, well built and very distinguished looking. His piercing blue eyes, neatly trimmed beard and beautiful hands, and his manner of dress made a great impression on people meeting him for the first time. Ugo Ojetti, a journalist and critic who knew Fortuny well, gives us this description of him: 'He is as simple and sober as an anchorite. He always wears summer clothes, even when the *bora* is blowing, always of the same colour and made from the same material: an Inverness cape of black cloth, a lightweight suit of dark blue serge, a white silk cravat, a black

Opposite: Cecilia Fortuny (above) seated in her husband's Roman studio. (Archivo Mas, Barcelona) Mariano's studio (below) on the first floor of the Palazzo Orfei in Venice. (Countess Elsie Lee Gozzi, Venice) The objects that Fortuny inherited from his father helped to strengthen the resemblance between the two rooms.

Mantlepiece in Fortuny y Marsal's studio. Mariano shared his father's passion for oriental and Arabic artifacts, drawing inspiration from them for his own motifs and designs. (Archivo Mas, Barcelona)

slouch hat, and low-heeled patent leather shoes or sandals of plaited red leather.'[6]

Fortuny had a horror of middle-men and disliked depending upon others. If a project became too large to be dealt with inside the Palazzo Orfei and he had to go outside for help, he generally found the experience disappointing. Unlike Morris, Fortuny did not attempt to achieve an artistic or social ideal, and was content to work in isolation away from the mainstream of events. The things that most interested him about the age in which he lived were the technological developments which he was able to adapt to his own purposes; he ignored all the modern artistic movements and dismissed the ideas of their major exponents.

He showed little interest in competing, in measuring himself against the achievements of others, in creating something new and original in the way this is understood by many artists of the twentieth century. Yet it would be foolish to assess Fortuny in the light of modern artists; he is simply a case apart. In his work, time in the sense of change and evolution does not exist in the usual way. There is a definite evolution and refinement of technique, but no formal development. He does not pass through different stylistic periods as other artists normally do. At the end of his life he was painting and engraving in exactly the same manner as he had done twenty years earlier, often making use of the same imagery, and it is thus almost impossible to date his work chronologically according to style or content. Even the products which he marketed, such as his fabrics and dresses, did not vary in their essential form: the pleated silk gown is a theme which he

repeated with subtle variations for over forty years.

If Fortuny's conception of time depended at least partially on his upbringing and the environment in which he lived, Venice and the Palazzo Orfei, the atemporal quality of his work was a direct result of the examples which inspired him: the art of the past and that of non-Western cultures where the concept of progress and change did not exist until the arrival of European colonists. From Egyptian art through to the end of the nineteenth century, everything was valid; any painting, sculpture, etching or detail thereof could provide a model, an idea which he could interpret and transform into something of his own. His favourite periods were Classical Greece, the Renaissance, and the great Venetian art of the fifteenth and sixteenth centuries which still surrounded him. Of all non-Western cultures, the one he preferred, perhaps out of love for his father, was the Arabic culture – during the era of its greatest expansion when it extended from Morocco to India passing through Persia and the Near East.

Fortuny was an eclectic, but this term, derogative for us, was not considered as such in earlier times. Mariano made unabashed use of traditional ideas to realize his dreams and projects, adapting them to his own aesthetic vision and producing objects and inventions which dazzled his contemporaries. Nowhere did his alchemy work greater wonders than in the field of fabric and dress design. It was here that Fortuny revealed the full scope of his genius, achieving a subtle synthesis of art and function, of technical ingenuity and taste, of past, present and future: creations which, in the words of Proust, remain 'faithfully antique but powerfully original'.[7]

A view of Venice in the 1890s. Mariano took this picture with a Kodak Panoram, the first camera to provide wide-angle photographs. He was an avid photographer who recorded every aspect of his life and work, assembling a library of over 10,000 negatives. (Museo Fortuny, Venice)

II

VENICE:
PAINTING, DRAWING, ENGRAVING

I have been interested in many things, but have always considered painting to be my profession.

MARIANO FORTUNY

The Venice of 1889 was no longer the rich and powerful city of previous centuries. Only thirty years had elapsed since it had been released from the Austrian yoke and incorporated into the newly formed Kingdom of Italy. Its personality was decided not by politics, commerce or art, but by the nostalgic beauty of its past, and the monuments which bore witness to its former glory. The French Symbolist poet Henri de Regnier, a frequent visitor, wrote:

> 'From all that she was and from all that she will never again be, Venice preserves a beauty which is made even more moving by a character that is at the same time one of decay and also of finality. From having lived through the whole span of life, from splendour to decrepitude, from zenith to decay, Venice has retained from this perfection of her destiny a dignity and a serenity. Her lost grandeur yields to familiarities. Her justifiable pride allows her to grant them without feeling in any way diminished.'[1]

This was the romantic Venice of Byron, Shelley, Heine, Alfred de Musset, Liszt, and Wagner. But artists, poets and musicians were not the only ones flocking to the city on the lagoon. There were ordinary travellers, adventurers, art collectors and connoisseurs, and of course wealthy tourists doing the Grand Tour. Many of them became enamoured of the place, taking up residence on a more permanent basis, and a foreign colony began slowly to establish itself. The early visitors were mostly English, but as the century progressed this élite group became less exclusive and more international.

The Fortunys' new home, the eighteenth-century Palazzo Martinengo

Mariano with an early camera, the Dubroni Stereograph. He regarded photography as more than an amusement, and made extensive use of the new medium for his paintings and textile designs. (Museo Fortuny, Venice)

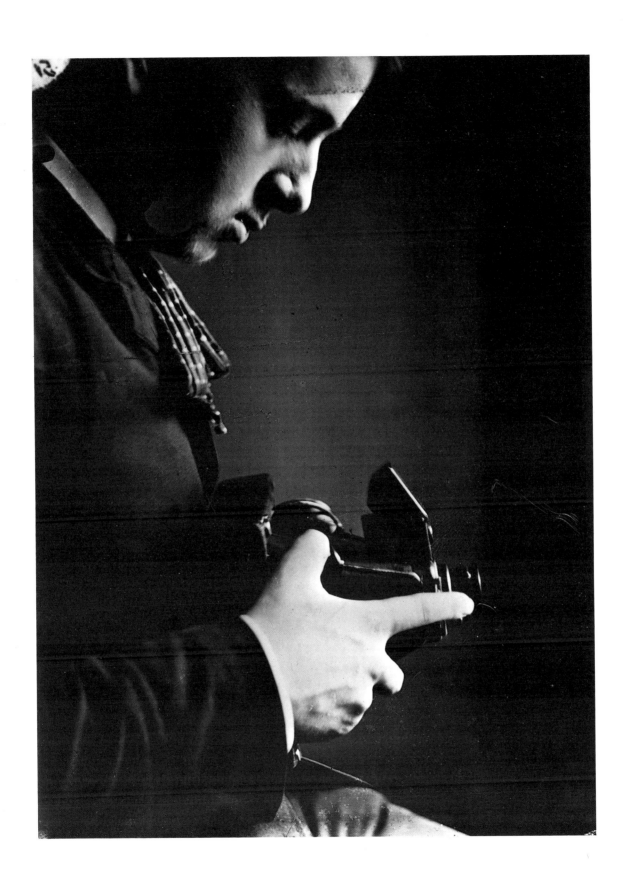

in San Gregorio, overlooked the Grand Canal near to where the latter flows into St Mark's Basin, and enjoyed marvellous views over the city and the lagoon. Nearby was the Palazzo Barbaro-Wolkof, home of the Russian intellectual painter and photographer Alexander Wolkof, and it was there that Eleonora Duse, resting after a theatrical tour of Europe and the United States, embarked on her passionate relationship with Gabriele D'Annunzio. Two doors away was the Venier dei Leoni, soon to be the home of the famous Marchesa Casati. Better known as the Palazzo Non Finito, it now houses the Peggy Guggenheim Foundation. On the other bank of the Grand Canal, almost opposite, stood the Casetta Rossa, once the studio of the Neo-classical sculptor Canova, which had been acquired several years previously

The Grand Canal of Venice photographed by Mariano soon after his family moved there in 1889. (Museo Fortuny, Venice)

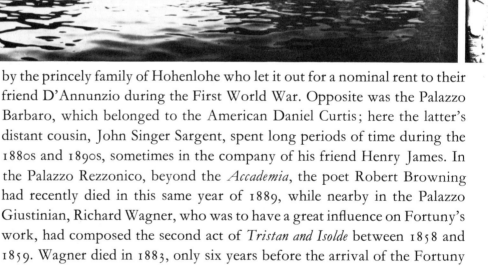

by the princely family of Hohenlohe who let it out for a nominal rent to their friend D'Annunzio during the First World War. Opposite was the Palazzo Barbaro, which belonged to the American Daniel Curtis; here the latter's distant cousin, John Singer Sargent, spent long periods of time during the 1880s and 1890s, sometimes in the company of his friend Henry James. In the Palazzo Rezzonico, beyond the *Accademia*, the poet Robert Browning had recently died in this same year of 1889, while nearby in the Palazzo Giustinian, Richard Wagner, who was to have a great influence on Fortuny's work, had composed the second act of *Tristan and Isolde* between 1858 and 1859. Wagner died in 1883, only six years before the arrival of the Fortuny family, in another *palazzo* also situated on the Grand Canal, the Palazzo Vendramin, to which he had returned in order to finish work on *Parsifal*.

This brief résumé of the illustrious inhabitants living along the Grand Canal gives a good idea of the mood of *fin-de-siècle* Venice. Around the owners of these *palazzi* there gravitated the floating population of friends, relations and artists who arrived in the city as their guests. Besides this group, which enjoyed a hectic social life, there were other visitors who either did not belong to that particular *milieu* or were not interested in its social aspect: students such as Ruskin, who had lived in the Pensione della Calcina in the Zattere (and also in the elegant Hotel Danieli), and his great rival Whistler who, although he normally loved socializing, came to the city to work. The result of Whistler's visit was to be his wonderful 1879 series of Venetian watercolours and etchings. Venice also attracted a number of Impressionists, such as Manet, Renoir, Le Sidaner and Walter Sickert and, at the beginning of this century, the French painter Paul Signac. 'It was not subjects that Venice gave fin-de-siècle painters – Delacroix had taken all too many, fifty years before – but colours used in a symbolic palette of alternately bright and dull ... of all those shades of mildew which we find again in

Left: Another, more intimate view of Venice by Fortuny. The way in which he 'framed' the subjects of his paintings and engravings owed much to his interest in photography. (Museo Fortuny, Venice)

D'Annunzio's "Il fuoco", and in Thomas Mann's "Death in Venice".'[2]

Above: The exterior of the Palazzo Martinengo at S. Gregorio, where Mariano lived with his mother and sister as a young man. His studio was on the top floor. (E. Momeñe)

The foreign colony reflected accurately what Venice represented at the time, being responsible for nearly all of the city's social, intellectual and artistic life. Some of these foreigners, such as the Hohenlohes – who were later forced to leave at the outbreak of the First World War – made a permanent home there, opening their doors to intellectuals and artists, both Venetian and non-Venetian; in their house, the famous Casetta Rossa, the Austrian Prince Frederick and his wife Zina established a meeting place in which 'it was possible to find assembled Goluchowsky and Kitchener, De Régnier and Rilke, La Duse and D'Annunzio, Origo and de Maria, a Princesse de Ligne and a Metternich princess, Hoffmannstahl and the Comtesse de Nouailles.'[3] It was there that Mariano met Gabriele D'Annunzio, the leading literary figure of his day and a man who would have a significant influence on Fortuny's career.

D'Annunzio met Fortuny in the autumn of 1894 on the poet's second trip to Venice when he also made the acquaintance of the famous actress Eleonora Duse. By this time he was already a well-known writer who had

María Luisa wearing a Spanish costume from the period of Goya. Mariano painted this portrait of his sister in 1895 when he was twenty-four. The family crest can be seen in the background. (Museo Fortuny, Venice)

published a number of books, amongst which were some of his most important novels, such as *Le Piacere* (*Pleasure*), *Le Trionfo della Morte* (*The Triumph of Death*) and *Vergini delle Rocce* (*Virgins of the Rocks*). An immediate *rapport* developed between the two men as a result of their shared interest in art and the theatre, and later that year, when the poet founded *Il Convito*, a literary magazine in the style of the English *Yellow Book* or the German *Pan*, he asked Mariano to illustrate it with one of his drawings. At the Hohenlohes Fortuny also met Angelo Conti, an administrator in the Venetian museums and an old friend of D'Annunzio. Conti later dedicated his essay on aesthetics and art, *La Beata Riva*, to Mariano with the following words: 'May this book, in which I see art as a bank along which flows the river of oblivion, serve to remind you of the faithful friend who loves you for the richness of your talent and the goodness of your will.'[4]

During this period of the 1880s Venetian art began to recover from the decline into which it had subsided after Canova had left the city in 1781. A whole series of important native-born artists began to emerge, men such as Luigi Nono, Ettore Tito, Alessandro Milesi, Francesco Sartorelli, Mario de Maria (better known as Marius Pictor), and Lino and Luigi Selvatico, many of whom exhibited in the Venetian International Exhibition in 1887. It was this artistic flowering that gave birth to the idea of organizing, every two years, an international art exhibition, the first of which took place in 1895. The series still continues today under the title of the Venice Biennale.

The eighteen-year-old Mariano had his studio on the third floor of the family *palazzo* and spent most of his time in close contact with his mother and his sister María Luisa, neither of whom showed any interest in joining the social élite: 'We are recluses here,' wrote Doña Cecilia in 1891, 'which worries us not at all, since this is such a happy house and we always have so much to do in it that time always passes swiftly and pleasantly.'[5] But they always kept open house, both for the Spanish colony and for other nationalities, particularly for artists. Martín Rico, a Spanish landscape painter who had fallen in love with Venice, and who had also been a great friend of the elder Fortuny with whom he had been painting in Granada when Mariano was born, was a frequent visitor, as were his compatriots Pradilla, Benlliure, and later Zuloaga and Sert. The English Impressionist painter Walter Sickert, who during his visits to Venice formed part of Doña Cecilia's salon, mentions these colourful meetings in a letter written to Jacques-Emile Blanche in around 1900: 'I am delighted with the Fortunys where I go every Sunday. A delightful polyglot tea with cakes and sweets and Xeres and fair Venetians. They are really charming people with a fascinating cordiality

Mariano with the Spanish painter Aureliano Berunete (fourth from the left) and his family at the Hotel Castilla in Toledo c. 1895. Ricardo de Madrazo (far left) is seated next to Berunete's wife. (Mariano de Madrazo, Spain)

which remains discreet and well-mannered. I wonder if all Spaniards are as charming.'[6]

Sickert was very much in love with Mariano's sister and contemplated marrying her. When Jacques-Emile Blanche remarked on this to Rafael Ochoa, a relation of the Fortunys on the Madrazo side, the latter replied that marriage with a woman with so many quirks and manias was impossible.[7] María Luisa, or 'Foubis' as she was known by the family, was nonetheless an original and entertaining personality. She played the piano and sang beautifully, particularly the works of Wagner, a passion for which she shared with Mariano. As a child she was evidently beautiful, but at this period, to judge by the portraits and photographs of her that have survived, she was not exactly the 'ravishing beauty and marvel of grace'[8] that she appeared to Sickert. It seems that losing her looks affected her greatly; she gave up music and began to develop a series of obsessions – never sleeping lying down but always upright in an armchair, never killing anything, not even insects – which became ever more numerous towards the end of her life. In 1893 Fortuny painted a portrait of her wearing a Spanish dress from the time of

Self-portrait of Fortuny in 16th century Venetian costume, 1887. Only sixteen when he painted this, Mariano already showed a love for classical styles of painting and dress. The accompanying photograph taken by the artist was used as a preliminary study. (Museo Fortuny, Venice)

Goya; he also photographed her frequently, either alone or with their mother.

When Mariano first arrived in Venice, he enrolled for night classes at the *Accademia*, not far from his home, in order to perfect his drawing technique. In 1892 he sent two '*Accademia*' studies to his grandfather, Federico Madrazo, who is reported to have liked them very much.[9] But Fortuny the artist was not the product of any painting academy, and even if he were heir to a great academic tradition, this heritage was not reflected in his finished works, since he rejected the academic concept of contrived perfection and polish. His technique developed rather in the different museums where he studied and copied the works of the Old Masters right up to his death. In 1893, for example, he copied a Tintoretto in the Prado, in 1925 Rubens' *Susanna and the Elders*, in 1935 a number of Tintorettos in Milan and Paris, and in 1945 he did a breathtaking copy of Tiepolo's *Pala d'Este*. These and other copies, many of which are dated, can still be seen in the present *Palazzo Fortuny*.

Copying the works of classical painters was part of the artistic education of every late nineteenth-century artist, and not simply the academic ones. Impressionists, such as Manet, Degas and Cézanne, and particularly Symbolists such as Gustave Moreau and Maurice Denis, all sought inspiration and technical knowledge from painters of the past. By the end of the century, however, a new means of spreading art both simply and extensively had arrived in the form of photographic reproduction. Fortuny's collection of reproductions was truly impressive. Not restricted exclusively to painting or artistic subjects, it was a vast archive containing every type of shape and form: archaeological remains, Roman amphitheatres, cathedrals, sculpture, painting and all the 'lesser' arts, as well as natural forms such as woods, mountains and plants. He organized all these photographs into perfectly classified albums, under titles such as 'windows', 'Greek heads', 'Roman amphorae', 'trees', 'mountains' and so on, and by the time he died they numbered almost a hundred volumes. Fortuny himself grouped his work as a painter into the following categories: portraits, stage designs, landscapes, compositions and decorative murals.

A. G. Temple, in his book *Modern Spanish Painting* written in 1908, says that Fortuny 'has latterly given his attention largely to portraiture', and other authors speak of him as a painter of female portraits, but we know of very few from this period. Fortuny's first self-portrait at the age of sixteen, dated 1887, shows him dressed in the sort of clothes one associates with a Titian portrait. The whole painting has a very Venetian feel to it; not only

Georgia Clementi photographed by Mariano at the turn of the century. One of Fortuny's first loves, she inspired many of his early paintings and etchings. (Museo Fortuny, Venice)

the costume but also the face in profile, the body shown in three-quarter length, the colours and even the open window leading to an indistinct land-scape in the distance. Yet the portrait is not based on any Titian prototype, but on a photograph that he probably took himself, in which he appears in the same pose dressed in contemporary clothes against a backdrop with no window. Fortuny used photography, which was then a very modern and revolutionary medium, to help him formulate his ideas quickly and as an aid in solving the problems of composition encountered in his paintings. Two other portraits from this period were also based on photographs, the one of his sister in 1893 and another of Princess Hohenlohe dated 1899. The princess – with whom he had, incidentally, become very friendly – appears

in a dress which, although it could be contemporary, recalls the fashions of the 1830s.

It was not a desire for historicism or a quirk of personality that made Fortuny change his contemporary clothes for sixteenth-century dress. Like many other artists of the time, he agreed with the painter George Frederick Watts when he said: 'Portraiture is deprived of nearly all, that from an artistic point of view, can render it valuable to posterity ... The ugliness of most things connected with our ordinary habits is most remarkable.'[10] This penchant for portraying and being portrayed in fancy dress, combined with a predilection for dressing up in different disguises, as can be seen in a number of his photographs, reveals a love and feeling for dress that is basic to our understanding of the Fortuny of later years: the designer of dresses and fabrics, both for the theatre and for everyday use.

Fortuny's portrait of Princess Hohenlohe was exhibited in Venice's Third International Art Exhibition in 1899, when he was twenty-seven, and was commented on with great interest by two of the most astute Italian critics of the day. Vittorio Pica wrote in *Emporium*, '... there is one by Mariano Fortuny, who I still cannot bring myself to consider as anything else but an Italian painter, a portrait of a woman, which shows a rare technical skill and a quality of delicate and fascinating elegance that brings to mind the English coloured engravings of the last century.'[11] Achille de Carlo remarked: 'The portrait exhibited by Fortuny, that of a woman in Empire dress, which subtly combines both feeling and charm, and which is a brilliantly evocative work, makes us bemoan his absence from Italian exhibitions.' [12]

Like his father, Fortuny was not fond of showing his work, even though he did so to a much greater extent during this early period. In 1896 he had exhibited one of his works in the International Exhibition in Munich, in 1899 he exhibited in the salon of the *Société Nationale des Beaux Arts* as well as in the Biennale, and in 1900 he showed them once more in the *Société Nationale* and also in the International Exhibition in Paris. In 1901 he exhibited in England, in the art gallery in the London Guildhall, and in 1902 he again exhibited in the *Société Nationale* in Paris; but it should be remembered that these were all group exhibitions, in which no more than two or three of his works would be shown. In fact, compared with his contemporaries, Fortuny had very few exhibitions.

Both of the critics mentioned above contrived in some way to relate Fortuny to the Italian school of art, but the truth of the matter is that he did not belong to a particular school or national art movement. On the other hand, Pica, who speaks of 'rare technical skill', was among the first to notice

Opposite: Photo-portrait of Princess Hohenlohe, which Fortuny used as the basis for a painting (inset) exhibited at the Venice Biennale of 1899. She also appears in the poster advertisement (below) that Mariano designed in the same period. The Hohenlohe palazzo on the Grand Canal was a famous meeting place for writers and artists at the turn of the century. (Museo Fortuny, Venice)

the hand of an alchemist in his work. Fortuny was a master craftsman who invented his own techniques and always placed great emphasis on the materials with which he was working. His was an idealistic, Aristotelian concept of art in which the artist's task is to discover the form inherent in the material. 'The best material for a work of art is the one that demands the most work,' wrote Fortuny in 1896. 'For example, 10 units of material that can contain not 10 but 100 units of creation, represents the peak of perfection in the achievement of a visibly transmissive quality in the work of art.'[13] This may explain why Fortuny began to make his own colours, which he later marketed with great success, and his continual striving to discover and perfect new materials for his creations.[14] 'Work is something active. There is no such thing as passive work. One part of visible work can depend on two parts of intellectual work, just as two parts of visible work can depend on one part of intellectual work. Visible work can immediately be recognized from the proportion of intellectual work on which it depends. No artifice can prevent any work from revealing its source. Work is a child that always recognizes its father.'[15]

At the same time as working in oils, gouache or tempera, Fortuny also did etching, aquatint and dry-point. In his opinion, one of the very 'best materials for a work of art' – because it demanded the most work – was the engraver's copper plate, and he cited Dürer's *Melancholy* as an example of its great potential.

Fortuny often dealt with the same subjects in both engravings and paintings; as well as his portraits, there is an important group of drawings, engravings and pictures dealing with the theme of woman, a subject that fascinated all *fin-de-siècle* painters. Fortuny's women had neither the symbolic imagery of the Symbolists nor the earthy quality of the Realists, yet they contained elements of both styles. If he worked in a realistic way, it was with an idealistic mentality; reality was his starting point, but in the process of creating his imagery he tended to embellish that reality, giving his women a mysterious and distant quality that occasionally relates them to the Symbolist concept of beauty. Unlike the Symbolists, however, Fortuny's women were never chimeras or supernatural creatures; they appear in their natural forms without special attributes, and always alone against a neutral background.

In a drawing from 1895, of the back of a woman, the most important element is her hair: in fact, the rest of the work is merely a pretext for its study. This stylization of the hair, together with the artist's monogram, similar to the signatures used by Whistler, Moore and Beardsley, was the result of Modernist influences. Hair for Mariano was an essential ingredient

Mariano's photographic collection contains numerous nude studies which he made over the years. (Museo Fortuny, Venice)

Charcoal drawing dated 1895 bearing Fortuny's monogram. The artist frequently portrayed women with long, tangled hair, which he made the principal decorative element in many paintings and engravings. (Biblioteca Nacional, Madrid)

of female beauty; it spoke its own language, a fetishistic and decorative language that the artist shared with the Symbolists. His women normally have long and flowing hair, tangled and anarchic, which sometimes – as in his 1896 engraving – covers their faces and gives them their personality.

Fortuny confronted his subject as a portraitist; his sole interest was the woman herself and her personal attributes, to which he had no desire to add any ornamentation or narrative element. This can be seen in *La Innominata*, which he exhibited in 1899 in the *Salon de la Société Nationale des Beaux Arts* in Paris, along with two other canvases, one of which, *Le Réveil*, also por-

Overleaf: Charcoal drawing of Henriette, Fortuny's wife and life-long assistant, c. 1900. (Biblioteca Nacional, Madrid)

à Elsie
Souvenir du Passé !!!
Henriette

trayed a woman. His women were not figments of his imagination: they existed in real life. His inspiration during these years was a woman by the name of Giorgia Clementi, who had the same kind of hair as the women in these early works.

Fortuny liked to depict voluptuous women, not as ample as those of Rubens, but in clear contrast to the pale and angular beauties of the Symbolists. His prototypes can be found once again in classical painting, particularly in the work of Titian, for whom hair was also a major decorative and expressive element.[16]

Venetian Woman in the Wind. *Fortuny used dentist drills for etching the background. (Calcografía Nacional, Madrid)*

There are a number of etchings which relate to the studies mentioned above, such as *The Venetian Woman in the Wind* and an unfinished etching of a woman's head, as well as a number of male studies: the head of a Cardinal, the Satyr, the rather Rembrandtesque rabbi, or his study of a male back, which is reminiscent of the work of Michelangelo. Other Fortuny etchings were inspired by his father's work. *The Little Satin Shoe* is reminiscent of the elder Fortuny's pictures, with figures dressed in eighteenth-century dress, and *The Spanish Saddle* recalls his genre paintings. *The Arab Sword*, however, was actually a design by his father which Fortuny completed after the latter's death; the hilt had already been engraved and Fortuny merely finished the composition. The elder Fortuny also inspired some of his son's flower studies. These exist in tempera and also as etchings – the latter being of much higher quality. The variegated shrubs, intermingled with roses, hollyhocks and other flowers, were taken from sketches done by his father during the last years of his life, like the one now in the Prado. In his treatment of flowers Fortuny removed himself completely from the ranks of the presupposed realists, creating free and imaginative compositions which probably bring him nearer to the Symbolist aesthetic than any other of his works.

The Arab Sword, *an etching begun by Fortuny y Marsal and completed by his son. The hilt had already been engraved when Fortuny y Marsal died. (Calcografía Nacional, Madrid)*

There are also a number of pencil portraits by Fortuny dating from this period, the most outstanding of which is of Henriette done at the turn of the century. The drawing, which is now in the *Biblioteca Nacional* in Madrid, was executed with very thick lines, serving to emphasize the fleshiness of the face and its features to a greater extent than in any other of his engravings or drawings.

Mariano met Henriette Negrin in 1897 during one of his frequent trips to Paris, and was obviously taken by the robust beauty of this young French-woman whom he immortalized in countless drawings and pictures over the following years. At first they saw each other only intermittently, whenever Fortuny was in the French capital, but by 1902 their relationship had developed to the point where they decided to live together on a more open

The remains of the famous bell-tower in St Mark's Square. Henriette's arrival in Venice on the day of its collapse in 1902 caused Doña Cecilia to see the event as an ill-omen.

and permanent basis. Already the artist's muse, Henriette was to become his faithful companion and invaluable assistant, remaining by his side right up until his death. Her arrival in Venice was not welcomed by Doña Cecilia, however, who regarded this *'petite bourgeoise'*, divorced from a former husband, as unworthy of her beloved 'Mano'. By an unfortunate coincidence, the collapse of the bell-tower in St Mark's Square – an event that shook the city to the core – occurred on the very day of her coming, and this was seized upon as a kind of ill-omen. Nor did Henriette find favour with María Luisa who, having performed a graphological analysis of her handwriting, failed to discover the kind of qualities she would have liked to see in a female companion of her brother.

It is probable that there was a deeper reason for the two ladies' antipathy towards Henriette, since her arrival also coincided with Mariano's final departure from the Palazzo Martinengo. Fortuny had a particularly intimate relationship with his mother and sister, and the bond between them was strengthened by the cult of art and the atmosphere of veneration for the memory of his famous father. They shared a world of dreams and recollections carefully preserved from ravages of time behind the insular walls of their Venetian palace.

The Palazzo Martinengo was a world of its own, suspended in time and space like the city in which it was situated. Brothers, sisters and other relatives of Doña Cecilia were frequent visitors, and the women loved to have interesting people for an afternoon to discuss art and literature, but nothing in substance was allowed to change, and as Henri de Régnier observed, 'The two Venetian ladies retained a very Spanish look'. Mariano's mother naturally encouraged him in his artistic endeavours and devoted considerable amounts of the family's money to her son's 'unremunerative' experiments, but depending upon her had obvious drawbacks. The time had come for Fortuny to break out of the secluded world of the Martinengo and establish his own identity.

The studio in his home was in any case becoming too small for his more ambitious projects, and by 1899 he had already transferred it to a couple of rooms in the Palazzo Orfei. There he installed a painting studio and workshops where he conducted experiments in finding the best pigments, as well as doing research into lighting and theatre design, both of which had begun to interest him in the early 1890s. The innumerable families that had divided up the Palazzo Orfei since the beginning of the century had thereby destroyed its architectural harmony and original decoration, so Fortuny, as he began taking over the building, also worked systematically on its restoration.

As work on the Orfei progressed, Mariano spent less and less time in his mother's house. He stopped attending the parties organized around Doña Cecilia and María Luisa in order to lock himself away with his experiments, and began transplanting, albeit unconsciously, some of the spirit of the Martinengo to his new home. The only thing lacking was a woman to look after it, and when this role was finally filled by Henriette, much to the distaste of the Fortuny women, it caused considerable tension between the Martinengo and the Orfei. On one hand, Doña Cecilia regarded living together out of wedlock as scandalous; on the other, she saw Henriette as taking her place in Mariano's life.

The Spanish Saddle, *an etching which recalls the genre paintings of Mariano's father. (Calcografía Nacional, Madrid)*

Henriette was rarely admitted into Doña Cecilia's presence and remained outside the private world of the Martinengo, but this was not enough to separate Mariano from his family and he regularly visited them on his own to share the results of his labours and discuss future projects. Although the couple eventually married many years later, Doña Cecilia never reconciled herself to Henriette or to the fact that Mariano had developed a life-style independent of her influence. Nonetheless, she maintained a fervent interest in her son's career.

One of Fortuny's main sources of inspiration was Richard Wagner. The legends that provided the basis for Wagner's musical dramas also furnished Fortuny with a vast range of images, which he, like many of his artist contemporaries, developed in his paintings and engravings. In addition, Wagner's whole *oeuvre* and his theories on theatre and art, which Fortuny was familiar with and admired greatly, provided the artist with an idealistic concept of the whole panorama of art, introducing him to the world of theatre, stage design and lighting.

Wagner and 'Wagnerianism' were essential elements of the *fin-de-siècle*, not only in art and literature, but in every aspect of culture, since Wagner was regarded with equal esteem as a musician, a poet and a philosopher. Despite the fact that he had died in 1885, his music and his other works continued to divide society, just as they had done during his lifetime, into Wagnerians and anti-Wagnerians. Everybody took sides: nobody was left unmoved by his work. Artists and poets were, on the whole, fervent Wagnerians, particularly the Decadents and Symbolists, and in the famous *Revue Wagnerienne*, illustrating the articles of Mallarmé, there appeared lithographs by Fantin-Latour, Odilon Redon, Jacques-Emile Blanche and Rogelio de Egusquiza who together with Aubrey Beardsley and the Belgian, Jean Delville, were the most important illustrators of Wagnerian myths and heroes.

As a young man Mariano was introduced to Wagnerian music and mythology by the Spanish painter Rogelio de Egusquiza,[17] who had been a personal friend of the German composer. Egusquiza lived in Paris, and it was there, thanks to his friendship with Doña Cecilia, that the young Fortuny heard him enthusing about Wagner, Bayreuth, the Ring and *Parsifal*. Fortuny was spellbound; Doña Cecilia and María Luisa shared his enthusiasm, and in 1892 all three went to Bayreuth, where Egusquiza introduced them to Cosima, the composer's widow, and the rest of the Wagner family. Fortuny's 'Wagnerian experience' was a decisive milestone in his career, introducing him to a new world of aesthetic possibilities. In Wagner's view, art fulfilled a basic need in life, and he therefore did not regard painting, sculpture or music as separate entities: art transcended and at the same time united all its constituent elements. As Fortuny himself said: 'Wagner created a union of all artistic means of expression. Nobody but he could bring once more to light what Michelangelo had achieved. Wagner has restored to painting and architecture their *raison d'être*, he has made their existence a vital necessity, and he has performed the miracle that he alone was capable of achieving.'[18]

For Wagner the final product of this synthesis was the *Gesamtkunstwerk*, the opera as he himself planned it. The traditional concept of opera, as expressed by Italian contemporaries such as Verdi and Puccini, was that of a juxtaposition of different elements – the orchestra, libretto, scenery, stage directions and singing – with the singing (*bel canto*) predominating at the expense of the other elements, which acted as its accompaniment. Wagner maintained that opera was only valid as a work of art if a perfect union could be achieved between music, poetry (the dramatic element) and painting (the stage sets). His desire was to interrelate the arts, overcoming traditional

Below: Etching of a Venetian calle, *one of the many small back streets that Mariano preferred over the grander, more monumental Venice frequented by tourists. (Calcografìa Nacional, Madrid)*

Right: Etching of a man's back. The pose is reminiscent of sketches by Michelangelo, the artist most admired by Fortuny. (Calcografía Nacional, Madrid)

Left: Etching of a scene from Act I of Wagner's Parsifal: *Gurnemanz leading Parsifal to the castle of the Knights of the Holy Grail under the watchful eye of Kundry. Fortuny repeated this theme in several paintings and engravings. (Calcografia Nacional, Madrid)*

Below: Etching of a scene from Act II of Siegfried, *another Wagnerian opera.*

classifications and formalist barriers in order to create a single Art which would recover its vitality and function, and thus make a genuine contribution to society.

Fortuny began painting Wagnerian pictures from the time of his first visit to Bayreuth. He showed them to his artist uncles who did not like them very much, but Doña Cecilia, in a letter to her father, rose to their defence: 'Naturally it is necessary to have been to Bayreuth and be very involved in the whole thing to appreciate them.'

The Rhinegold, the first work of the Tetralogy, is in fact the prologue for the trilogy formed by *The Valkyrie*, *Siegfried* and *Twilight of the Gods*, and it is from *The Rhinegold* that Fortuny produced some of his best engravings. One of the most dramatic moments of the Tetralogy depicted by Fortuny is from *The Valkyrie*: a tempera painting of the passionate embrace between Sigmund and Sieglind as the curtain falls at the end of Act I. Among the most interesting of Fortuny's Wagnerian works, however, is his unfinished etching *The Fiery Incantation*, showing the final scene of *The Valkyrie* in which Wotan puts Brünhilde into an enchanted sleep on a rock surrounded by fire, as a punishment for her disobedience. It portrays the moment when Wotan invokes the god of fire: at the last call he strikes three times with his spear on the rock, from which a stream of fire springs forth. This quickly grows to a sea of flames which Wotan directs to encircle the rock.

> 'He who my spear-point's
>
> Sharpness feareth
>
> Shall cross not the flaming fire!'

The work ends with this spell that only Siegfried will be able to break.

Parsifal was Wagner's last work, the most mystical and also the favourite of both its composer and illustrators alike. It was based on the Arthurian legend of the Knights of the Round Table, but Wagner changed the original story to make Parsifal the hero, exalting his virtues of purity and faith and making him Titurel's successor as Keeper of the Holy Grail. Fortuny portrayed several scenes from *Parsifal*. From Act I he did two gouaches, two tempera paintings, three etchings and an engraved plate. From Act II came *The Flower Maidens*, a picture painted in 1896, which Fortuny showed in the International Exhibition in Munich that year, and which won him a Gold Medal. He also exhibited it in 1901 at the Guildhall in London. The picture shows Parsifal's encounter with the flower maidens in the enchanted garden of Klingsor, where they crowd adoringly around him

Etching of a scene from Shakespeare's Merchant of Venice. *Fortuny often transferred the same subject from one medium to another (see illustration on p. 52). (Calcografía Nacional, Madrid)*

until the appearance of Kundry puts them to flight. In the frame of the painting are written the words of the song with which the flower maidens hope to seduce Parsifal. It is one of Fortuny's most decorative works, and the one that comes closest to the Symbolists. Its stylization and the predominance of curves, both in the natural elements and the dresses, as well as in the overall composition, relate it to the 'poster aesthetics' of Modernism.

From Act III of *Parsifal* came Fortuny's two etched versions of Parsifal praying, in which he placed his central character in a strange landscape so as to give the necessary grandeur to this moment when Parsifal falls silently to his knees to pray before the Sacred Spear that has fallen into the hands of the magician Klingsor. Also from Act III are two tempera paintings and an engraving that show the Knights of the Grail in their white tunics, some bearing Titurel's bier and others carrying Amfortas' litter. In the two tempera paintings the cortège proceeds along a twisting path between high mountains, whilst in the engraving the Knights are shown in the foreground, with the countryside merely hinted at behind.

Wagner considered light to be a fundamental ingredient of his work, and countless artists endeavoured to express this mysterious and highly personalized element. Redon treats it as something formless, like a mist that envelops Parsifal and emphasizes his features and his dark eyes, hanging in the air like an indefinable backcloth. In Delville's poetic compositions this light becomes astral: from his *Parsifal* it emanates like rays of energy. Fortuny's light is nearer to that of Redon, but it is much more irregular and confused, with neither the tranquillity nor the immobility of Redon's *Parsifal*. Fortuny shows us Wagnerian scenes in a direct way, with an expressive quality that relates with great originality to both the legend and the idealism of the German composer.

An interesting part of Fortuny's work was based solely on the imaginary world, a world peopled by sirens, sea-monsters and giants, similar to that of the German artist Arnold Böcklin (1827–1901). Böcklin was a painter who exercised a strong thematic influence on the Decadents, but he himself retained an academic-realist technique, based on Baroque and Renaissance painters, which precluded the search for their particular brand of ambiguous and idealized beauty. In this sense Fortuny was very similar to Böcklin, whom he regarded as one of the great artists of the nineteenth century. Böcklin's obsession with water is reflected in Fortuny's etchings *Mermaid and Shell* and *Mermaid and Sea-Monster*, both of them unfinished. There are also two bronze reliefs of the same subjects, as well as two large versions in tempera done years later. Fortuny never considered any subject

Etching of a Jewish rabbi. (Calcografía Nacional, Madrid)

closed. He had to return to it, repeat it and study it in different materials, often ignoring the fact that many years had passed since the original version.

The Nordic myths on which Wagner based his works gave birth to a whole iconographic revival of giants, dragons, primeval gods and warriors. The latter elements became subjects that were used, sometimes outside a Wagnerian context, by idealist painters such as Böcklin – the artist whom Wagner himself would have liked to paint the scenes of the Tetralogy – and they became popularized by such illustrators as Arthur Rackham and Kay Nielsen. Fortuny, however, generally preferred less complicated and sensational scenes; his notes explain why.

> 'It is possible to have a work created in an instant that may completely satisfy the intellect of its author ... in which case, either it represents a long period of intellectual work, or it becomes a "motif", no more or less than a product of nature. Sublime art, such as that of Wagner or Michelangelo, is extremely rich in motifs, so much so that any fragment of their works, however small, is as large as any other, because it offers a motif, and whatever that may be, whether the wing of a mosquito or an enormous mountain, in no way will the one be greater than the other.'[19]

Fortuny constantly returned to Wagnerian themes, almost as if he had fallen under a spell cast by the German composer. Besides the paintings and engravings based on Wagner's works, he also did a considerable number of set designs over the years.

Landscapes, particularly Venetian ones, were a constant element in Fortuny's artistic production. During this early period his pictures and engravings reveal his gradual discovery of Venice, frequently in the company of his friends Angelo Conti and D'Annunzio. Fortuny's Venice is not the monumental Venice of Canaletto and Turner, nor is it the Venice of the Impressionists, such as Monet and Renoir, or of Whistler, all of whom tended to encapsulate the magic of the city in the grandeur of St Mark's or the Lagoon. Fortuny disassociated himself from this concept of the city in his search for a much more intimate Venice: the Venice of the connoisseur, the Venice of the Venetians. He was interested in the mundane but mysterious reality of its nooks and crannies, its forgotten canals, its narrow alleyways, its *sottoportici*, the houses with washing hanging from their balconies, the famous Venetian cats, and the sun and shade that played on the walls of the houses of the poor. The only aspect of St Mark's that appealed to him was its interior and the narrow glimpses of the *piazza* that could be gained through its half-opened door.

Overleaf:
4 tempera paintings on panel by Mariano set against a printed cotton of his own design; the pomegranate was inspired by a 15th century Renaissance motif.
Above: Nude 1888, similar to nude studies by Alexandre Cabanel and other 'pompier' painters.
Centre: 2 Carpaccio copies by Fortuny.
Below: Scene from The Merchant of Venice *c. 1913 (Museo Fortuny, Venice/E. Momeñe)*

A corner of the salon-studio in the Palazzo Fortuny, hung with Mariano's copies of Old Masters. (Museo Fortuny, Venice/E. Momeñe)

Unfinished etching entitled Mermaid and Sea-Monster. *Fortuny's imaginary world was inspired by the German painter Arnold Böcklin for whom Mariano had great admiration. (Calcografía Nacional, Madrid)*

Venetian street taken with Mariano's Kodak Panoram. The deep shadows and wide-angle distortion give this scene an almost surrealistic feeling. (Museo Fortuny, Venice)

The seemingly random way in which Fortuny's subjects are framed in the enclosed, sometimes claustrophobic spaces of etchings such as *Corner of a Canal*, *Alley and Kitten* and *Window and Cat* can only be explained in terms of photography, which he had discovered in Paris during the late 1880s. He learned to see Venice in a highly personal way through the hundreds of photographs that he had taken since his arrival, both outside and in his studio. There is one particularly interesting series of photographs of Venice from this period, which Fortuny took with a technically revolutionary camera that had just been brought out – the Kodak Panoram. This camera had a lens which, as soon as the shutter release was activated, began to turn on a spindle so that the whole image 'seen' by it was transferred on to the plate; the result was comparable to that achieved by modern wide-angle lenses, with a similar distortion of perspective. Mariano regarded photography as more than an amusement; it was a new medium with which he could create and experiment, as well as document the objects and experiences that were useful to him as an artist. He also took endless pictures of his family and friends, which provide an illuminating record of their daily life in Venice. By the end of his life he had accumulated a stock of over ten thousand negatives.

Fortuny's taste in painting was eclectic. Those whom he regarded as the best nineteenth-century painters often represented conflicting artistic currents and visions, such different man as Böcklin and Burne-Jones, Degas and Daumier or Ingres and Manet, not to mention his father and the Madrazo family. This reluctance to commit himself to any side of the argument raging through the art world at the turn of the century was bound to affect the quality of his own paintings. Rather than resolve the conflict, Fortuny chose to remain outside of it, modelling himself on the Old Masters, and ignoring the innovations of his time. Perhaps because of this, his painted *oeuvre* remains the least mature and interesting aspect of his work.

As an engraver, however, he managed to express himself with far greater effect. His engravings have a strength, a subtle delicacy and a feeling of mystery that is missing from many of his paintings, which sometimes show an extravagant, even strident use of colour and a poor treatment of form. This is very well illustrated by a comparison of either of the two engraved versions of the scene in which Parsifal is led by Gurnemanz to the castle, and their painted equivalent.

The copper plate, which he personally regarded as an ideal medium for a work of art, demanded a special effort that was well suited to his temperament. The true engraver is a mixture of artist and artisan who invents his

own methods. The same urge that drove Fortuny to make his own pigments led him also to develop his own etching technique; he used drills and other dentist's tools to produce those mournful and mysterious backgrounds in which the acid bit unevenly into the plate. It was a perfect means of expressing the unreal atmosphere of Venetian canals or Wagnerian scenery. These instruments also produced a black, velvety quality that resembles the effect achieved in a mezzotint. The procedure for making the plates was straightforward: the copper was chosen and drawn upon, then placed in an acid solution, and once the plate was ready it was tinted. Although Fortuny pulled his own prints on the hand-press which he kept in his library, few of them have survived. The plates, however, were bequeathed by his widow to the Royal Academy of Fine Arts in Madrid where occasionally new prints are still made from them.

The knowledge which Fortuny gained from a lifetime of painting and engraving was crucial to the development of his other activities. Through painting he learned the subtle uses and combinations of colour that would enable him in later years to produce the inimitable silks and velvets from which he made his exquisite garments. Through painting he also discovered the importance of light and the ways of using it to produce dramatic effects. Thus 'painting', in the sense that Fortuny conceived of it, was not simply a method of producing a picture, but rather an underlying aesthetic attitude in which colour and light played dominant roles.

It was this 'painterly', sensual, lavish mentality which led Fortuny, as it did artists of the Baroque period, to perceive the world in theatrical terms. The Palazzo Orfei was a natural stage-set where the artist conducted daily investigations into the properties of light, and from there it was but a small step into the proper world of stage-lighting and theatre design. The catalysts for this next step were once again Wagner and Bayreuth.

Overleaf:
The Embrace of Sigmund and Sieglind from Act I of Wagner's The Valkyrie (left). Tempera on canvas. Fortuny made a smaller version on board dated 1896, and a bronze statuette. (Museo Fortuny, Venice)

The Flower Maidens (right), from Act II of Wagner's Parsifal, was one of Mariano's most accomplished paintings. Dated 1896, it was awarded the Gold Medal at the International Exhibition in Munich that year. (Museo Fortuny, Venice/E. Momeñe)

MARIANO FORTVNY Y MADRASO

III

STAGE-LIGHTING AND
THEATRE DESIGN

*Theatrical scenery will be able to transform itself in tune with music,
within the latter's domain, that is to say in 'time,' whereas hitherto it
has only been able to develop in 'space.'*

MARIANO FORTUNY

In Bayreuth Fortuny's eyes were opened by Wagner to the possibilities and
needs of the theatre; thereafter he stopped devoting himself exclusively to
the fine arts and began exploring other avenues. During these years, the
early 1890s, the costumes and scenery of the Tetralogy and of Wagner's
other works were those that the composer had used during his lifetime.
Cosima Wagner ensured that everything remained just as her husband had
planned it, with the result that, fifteen years later, the same scenery was being
used in the Tetralogy as had been used for its first performance in the
presence of Ludwig II of Bavaria in 1876.

The stage sets were painted in a realistic manner, using antiquated
methods that disappointed Fortuny just as they had the Swiss stage designer
Adolphe Appia ten years earlier. The contradiction between this naturalistic
scenery and the spiritual or metaphysical music of Wagner was completely at
odds with the spirit of *Gesamtkunstwerk*, and Appia had already looked into
ways of bringing the scenery up to date. Fortuny appears to have been
similarly affected, for around 1893, only a year after his first visit to Bayreuth,
he began his first experiments with light and its effects.

During the latter part of the nineteenth century, light had been transformed through the harnessing of electricity. Suddenly the mystic light of
the cathedrals, the sensual light of the Venetian *palazzi* and the mysterious
light of the gaslit streets became full of new possibilities. In the great international exhibitions of the time the many practical applications of Edison's
invention were displayed and promoted. At the Paris Exhibition of 1889,
which Edison himself attended, the symbolic role of the Eiffel Tower as the

*Fortuny in his work clothes. Self-
portrait c. 1902. (Countess Elsie Lee
Gozzi, Venice)*

Fortuny's machine for testing his indirect stage-lighting system. A scale model of the required stage set, in this case a mountain view, was set in position and different skies produced by projecting light onto painted surfaces. (Museo Fortuny, Venice/E. Momeñe)

most impressive example yet of man's scientific and engineering achievement was greatly enhanced by electric light. By 1900 electricity was taking over, and several companies were offering to install the new power wherever it was wanted: in factories, hotels, workshops and even in private dwellings. Nor was its potential overlooked by the artists of the day. As Fortuny himself exclaimed some years later: 'Do you know of any mystery more beautiful than electricity?'[1]

This revolutionary new type of light had obvious possibilities as a means of stage-lighting. Until then gas had been used for lighting theatrical productions, but its function had been merely to emphasize the painted skies, clouds, woods, ruins and so on which formed the basis of stage scenery at the time. This type of scenery, however, had begun to grow stale, as had the theatre in general. It was not surprising therefore that the innovative years of the late 1890s brought with them a new type of stage design. No longer were stage sets of rooms composed of pieces of board painted to represent walls, windows and curtains: real tapestries, tables and chairs were used instead. If a scene took place in a butcher's shop, people did not hesitate to drag real sides of beef on stage and cut them up there and then, following the author's stage directions to the letter, while at the same time simplifying the scenery. The chief exponent of this type of set was Antoine with his *théâtre libre*; a similar line was taken by the *Freie Bühne* of Otto Brahm and Beerbohm Tree in Germany and the *Malyi Teatr* in Russia, but, as Ferruccio Marotti noted, 'it was not a course that could be followed far: within the concept of naturalistic scenery were planted the seeds of inevitable decay. Theatrical adornment very soon became a mechanical furnishing process, a sterile philological work, which within the space of a few years degenerated once more into a stale routine. The new staging technique needed to develop in non-imitative ways, like those which were being intuitively achieved by avant-garde painters and sculptors.

It was Adolphe Appia and the Englishman, Gordon Craig, who finally brought about this revolution in the theatre: Appia through studying the theories and contradictory results of Wagner's stage designs, and Craig as a result of his personal knowledge of the theatre, gained through being the son of the actress Ellen Terry and the architect, theatrical producer and stage designer Edward William Godwin, and also being himself an actor. Both men realized the importance of lighting in the theatre and the need to reform existing lighting methods. In accomplishing this reform, the practical participation of Fortuny was a vital element, running parallel to Appia's theoretical work during the 1890s. In his book *La Musique et la Mise*

Opposite: The Eiffel Tower, built for the Paris Exhibition of 1889, became a symbol of man's technological achievements. This role was enhanced by Edison's then recent discovery of the electric light which illuminated the structure. (Bibliothèque Nationale, Paris)

Below: Diagram of a movable arc-light with motor drive, which Fortuny patented in 1905. (Office National de la Propriété Industrielle, Lyon)

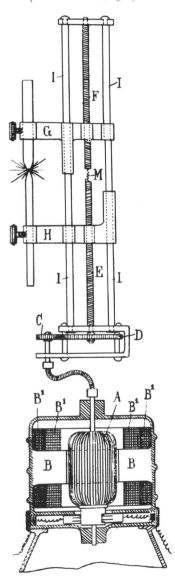

en Scène (Music and Stage Production), published in 1897, Appia wrote that 'light has the same function in representational terms as music has in the score: it is the expressive element opposed to the visible; and just like music, it can express nothing that is not an integral part of the essential elements of vision.'[3] This analogy between music and light, both of them abstract elements, was also expressed by Fortuny when he wrote: 'theatrical scenery will be able to transform itself thanks to light in tune with music, within the latter's domain'.[4]

Appia prepared a plan for a production of *The Ring of the Niebelung*, altering the picturesque realism of Wagner's stage sets, and presented it at Bayreuth. But Bayreuth, under the influence of Cosima Wagner, closed its doors to Appia, who was regarded as a sacrilegious intruder; the only proposal of his that they adopted was to change the gas lighting to electricity. However, changing one system of lighting for another does not achieve much if it is not accompanied by a change in mentality. As Fortuny wrote:

> 'People contented themselves with replacing gas, that is to say a naked flame, with the electric light bulb, without taking into any account the immense advantage of mobility that electricity allowed for in stage-lighting; they restricted themselves, as far as positioning was concerned, to doing electric lighting schemes in the same way as gas ones, which meant that electricity, which should have completely revolutionized the art of stage décor, left it in virtually the same state as before. In fact, apart from its strength, it was no improvement on the old methods.'[5]

As it happened, Fortuny was the first to make use of the opportunities presented by electricity, and the techniques he invented helped to revolutionize stage-lighting. Although he was not a reformer in the total way of Appia or Craig, who were professionals dedicated solely to the theatre and its reform, all three men pursued the same goal – to give new life and meaning to the theatre. Fortuny's contribution lay in the fact that his methods made possible the new theories expounded in Wagner's *Gesamtkunstwerk* (*The Universal Art*) and Appia's *Worttondrama* (*Word-Music Drama*). Since Fortuny was first and foremost a painter, it was logical that light was the theatrical element that fascinated him most and the one through which he was to bring about changes in the theatre. One of the basic advantages of his new stage-lighting system was, in his words, that 'it permits the artist to mix his colours on the stage, to paint in the theatre as if with a palette'.[6] He saw the stage as a three-dimensional picture and regarded himself as a 'painter of stage sets' rather than a set designer.

Two scale models for projected stage sets c. 1907: a production entitled St Mark's Basin *(above); and a play by Hoffmanstahl (below), whom Fortuny met in Berlin through Max Reinhardt. Neither project was realized. (Museo Fortuny, Venice/E. Momeñe)*

Fortuny began his research into lighting and the theatre in his attic studio in the Palazzo Martinengo, and in his 1904 treatise, *Eclairage Scénique* (*Stage Lighting*) he relates how quite by chance he made the discovery that formed the basis of his indirect light technique, a system which he patented in 1901 and constantly refined.[7]

> 'If one lets a ray of sunlight into a darkened room, one will see a shaft of light piercing the air, but the room will not be lit up. If one then introduces a white leaf of paper in front of this shaft, the light will break up and illuminate the whole room; and yet the actual quantity of light entering still remains the same in both cases. This experiment proves that it is not the quantity, but the quality of light that makes things visible and allows the pupil of the eye to open properly.'[8]

If instead of natural light an artificial light source is used, the result is the same, but with the advantage that the quantity of light can remain constant or be varied at will; the source is also movable and there is the possibility of using lights of different colours. Fortuny was in no doubt as to the superiority of the white light of the arc lamp over the yellow light of the gas lamp. The latter was still used for stage-lighting because electric light posed certain problems, but these Fortuny set out to resolve. He tried reflecting the light off a white surface, as in his original experiment, and achieved an effect similar to that of daylight, making it possible to light any object. He then discovered that if this light were shone on to a surface which was not white but multi-coloured, and which could be moved up to or away from the light source at will, the reflected light would take on the same colours and also be controllable in its intensity. This discovery meant that it was now possible to achieve infinite degrees of dimness and brightness, as well as a vast range of colours which could change almost imperceptibly from one to the other. The advantages of this kind of stage-lighting were enormous. As it produced a diffused light, it did not cut the scenery into sections but moulded it into a coherent whole, while the endless variety of colours which could be obtained by simply changing the reflective surface meant that all manner of different effects could be achieved: 'thus the colour is given a kind of score, just like the music'.[9] The stage manager at the controls was able to 'paint' the stage as he wished, choosing different effects and mixing them to his own formula.

Since it was projected from further away, this colour-reflected light transformed the stage by overcoming the main drawback of traditional sets: the empty, unlit spaces between sections of scenery which, so as not to

Mariano back-stage with an electrician c. 1906, at the time of his association with the German electrical firm A.E.G., which installed the Fortuny dome and lighting system in a number of European theatres. (Museo Fortuny, Venice)

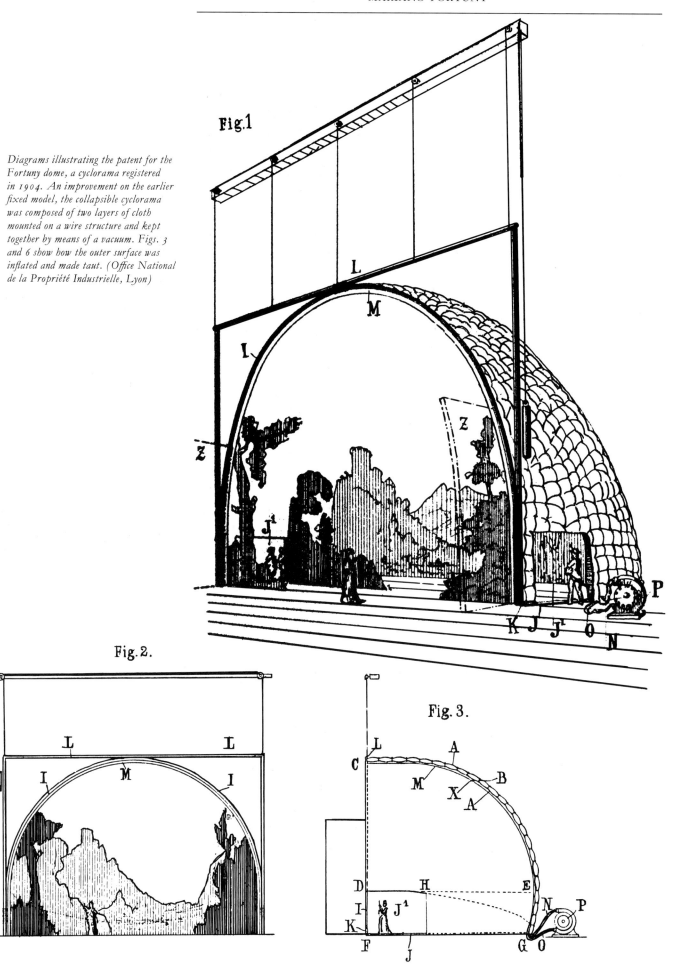

Fig.1

Diagrams illustrating the patent for the Fortuny dome, a cyclorama registered in 1904. An improvement on the earlier fixed model, the collapsible cyclorama was composed of two layers of cloth mounted on a wire structure and kept together by means of a vacuum. Figs. 3 and 6 show how the outer surface was inflated and made taut. (Office National de la Propriété Industrielle, Lyon)

Fig.2.

Fig. 3.

destroy the theatrical illusion, had hitherto been covered by more scenery, thereby creating an extremely complicated and cluttered effect, particularly in the area of the sky. With Fortuny's new system it was possible to achieve every conceivable sky effect by reflecting the coloured lights on to a cylindrical screen. The large numbers of painted backcloths used to represent skies during the day, at night, in the dawn or at dusk, which had to be constantly changed and which, however well they were managed, always interrupted the dramatic flow of the work in progress, were now replaced by the new form of lighting. Not only did this make stagecraft a much simpler procedure, it also represented a considerable saving in labour and costs.

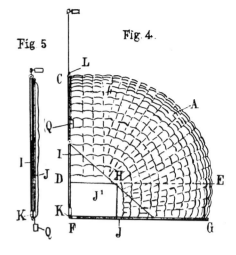

Fig 5   Fig. 4.

This preoccupation with simplifying the way in which the sky was represented and achieving the best effect possible led Fortuny to change the surface on which the lights were reflected. Hitherto this had been cylindrical (the panorama of Taylor and Soudiac), but it now became cylindrospherical, like a quarter globe, symbolizing the 'celestial vault' that it resembled. This was the first version of the famous Fortuny dome, a cyclorama situated at the back of the stage which served both as a backdrop and as a screen that exploited all the possibilities of indirect light. Fortuny put the finishing touches to his 'celestial vault' by engineering a system of small mirrors on which he painted groups of clouds; when he projected the coloured light on to these mirrors it reflected on to the dome, covering it with the image of the clouds. All the stage manager had to do was to wield the controls in order to produce a beautiful blue sky which, at the appropriate time, would suddenly become covered with clouds, and these in turn would yield to a sunset, and so on.

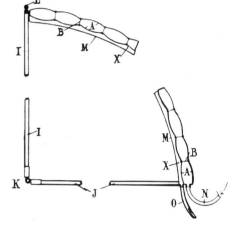

Fig. 6.

Although this new system did not completely do away with painted backcloths, it made staging much easier. As Fortuny wrote:

> 'Let us suppose that we are dealing with the second scene of *The Rhinegold* – its landscapes, panoramas, borders, side-scenes, side-drops, etc., need between 75 and 100 pieces of scenery, depending on the theatre; apart from those depicting the landscape and the mountain in the distance, all the others are there solely to conceal the backdrop. With my system and my celestial vault, the amount of scenery is limited to the number of pieces strictly needed to represent the subject ... four or five pieces would be enough for this scene, the illusion achieved by my lighting doing the rest.'[10]

There were other practical advantages: fewer stage hands were needed, while the fact that less scenery was involved meant less storage space and less danger of fire. Most important of all, however, it opened the way for stage design based on lighting, a concept that is still being developed in the modern theatre today.

'To sum up, my system is composed of three parts: – a system of lighting by means of reflection; – a system of stage decoration by means of reflection, allowing for the use of a concave surface to make skies and distant views; – last, and most important, a complete reform of the visual element in the theatre, because it can be said for the first time that theatrical scenery will be able to transform itself in tune with music, within the latter's domain, that is to say in 'time', whereas hitherto it has only been able to develop in 'space'. This last ability is of supreme importance for the staging of the works of Richard Wagner.'[11]

To understand what Fortuny meant all one has to do is to leaf through the careful stage directions in Wagner's works. In the first scene of *The Rhinegold*, for example, which takes place at the bottom of the Rhine, one reads: 'Greenish twilight, lighter above, darker below ...', or in the third scene of the final act of *Siegfried*: 'The clouds have dissolved into a fine rose-coloured veil of mist which now divides so that the upper part entirely disappears above and at length discovers the whole bright sky of day, whilst on the border of the rocky height now becoming visible a light veil of reddish morning mist ...'[12] Light is the essential ingredient of such scenes, and all Wagner's works require, in order to reproduce them faithfully, the use of a lighting technique that had until then remained undiscovered. It was Fortuny who showed the way.

During this period there was an upheaval in the Italian theatrical world, initiated by people like Eleonora Duse and Gabriele D'Annunzio, whose aim was to rescue their country's theatre from the mediocrity into which it had fallen. They formed a plan for a National Theatre on the outskirts of Rome near Lake Albano, a sort of Latin Bayreuth. D'Annunzio had recently become a great patriot, and this scheme was to be the first step in restoring his country to its former glory. He wanted the theatre to regain the mysterious and ceremonial character of Greek tragedy, which – together with works by him and other contemporary artists – would be performed in wild and natural surroundings, thereby recalling the rural, Dionysiac origins of drama. His notion of an amphitheatre which would house this dramatic revival was in some respects similar to Appia's theories on the reform of theatrical buildings as defined in *La Musique et la Mise en Scène* (*Music and Stage Production*) published during that same year. Both, in their own way, spoke of a new, open type of building based on Greek models, which in later years

Reflector lamp patented by Fortuny in 1903. The invention was based on the same principle as the cyclorama, reflecting diffuse light off a concave surface. The Paris design firm Ecart reissued the original Fortuny model in 1979. (Museo Fortuny, Venice)

was to influence Fortuny's designs for a theatre.

D'Annunzio, aware of Fortuny's experiments, became fascinated with the possibilities of indirect light and sought his cooperation. According to Gino Damerini, the first theatrical collaboration between the poet and the artist occurred in 1898: 'at the request of the poet and Sarah Bernhardt, he [Fortuny] prepared the sketch used for the scenery in the fifth act of *La città morta* in Paris.'[13]

Mariano Fortuny, the inventor, c. 1900.

The following year they met again in Venice. Fortuny had been commissioned by La Scala in Milan to do sketches for the sets of *Tristan and Isolde*, the première of which was scheduled for January 1901. At last he had been given the chance to put his ideas into practice in a work by Wagner, his master and inspiration. He was fully aware of the work's significance and also of the need to fuse music, poetry and painting in the performance. In addition, he knew its subject by heart. This would have been an ideal opportunity for him to exploit the full potential of his new system of indirect lighting and realize all his theories, both artistic and mechanical, but unfortunately it was impossible to transform the antiquated and complex stage mechanics of La Scala, and install the new system that Fortuny had just finished testing; he was only able to use a few simple effects that involved no alterations to the existing system.

This was not the only occasion on which his projects were to be thwarted by the restrictions of conventional theatres, but he always managed to temper his frustrations with a wry sense of humour. Remarking on the vagaries of the stage crew to a visiting journalist in 1932, he said:

> 'Why do electricians have to exist? Why don't they get arrested before a performance? For a short while only, of course! Until midnight would be enough. That would give us time to do things really well. During rehearsals, when they are absent-minded, I sometimes succeed in seeing my dream come true, but afterwards it is all back again to what it was before. Enough to make one desperate.'[14]

Nevertheless, his sets for *Tristan and Isolde* proved a great success. The critic in the magazine *Emporium* wrote: 'A young and fervent Wagnerian, who does credit to the glorious name of one of the century's most brilliant painters, M. Fortuny, painted the preliminary sketches for three sets of scenery and then lovingly realized their production; by virtue of their architectural elegance, their harmonious use of colour, their skilful portrayal of perspective and their realistic appearance, they can, and should be considered as true works of art.'[15] The artistic-literary review *La Lettura*,

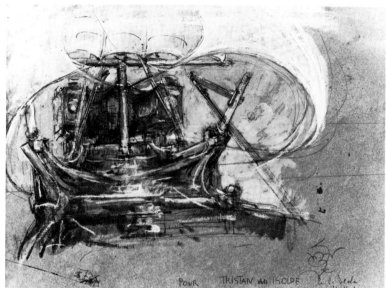

Set designs for Act I of Tristan and Isolde *performed at La Scala, Milan in 1901. Gouache (right), watercolour (centre) and photograph of completed set (far right). (Museo Fortuny, Venice)*

edited in Milan, devoted a whole article to the sets, analysing the potential of indirect light, Fortuny himself and his abilities as an interpreter of Wagner's work: 'Mariano Fortuny is really the only artist to devote himself to painting scenery, who has brought a feeling of art, a literary flavour, an instinctive genius to a *genre* that has hitherto been treated, with varying degrees of ability, as simply a trade.'[16]

Although Fortuny's sets involved a sparing use of materials and the absence of any unnecessary props, he never deviated from the stage directions contained in the text. His knowledge of the work's dramatic content gave his scenery an inherent quality that simplified the work both of the stage manager and the performers. In addition, he succeeded in involving the audience directly in the action. In the first scene of *Tristan*, for example, which Wagner describes as taking place in 'a pavilion on the deck of a ship, extensively decorated with magnificent fabrics', Fortuny placed the audience directly within the pavilion which embraced the whole stage, giving a cross-section of the ship's deck but allowing the spectator to catch glimpses of masts and rigging in the background. In this way he conveyed to the audience the impression that they were on board the ship without having to include its outline as traditional stage designers had done.

At the turn of the century Fortuny divided his working life between Venice and Paris where he hired a studio and spent long periods perfecting his lighting system and the prototype of his dome. In 1901 he was asked by D'Annunzio to design the scenery for a new work, *Francesca da Rimini*, on which the poet was working at the time. D'Annunzio wanted the production

to be realistic and expressive, as well as grandiose. It called for extremely complicated scenery, with effects such as smoke, boiling oil and so on to represent sieges and battles, and for costumes and sets with a high degree of historical authenticity. These strict requirements involved an extensive correspondence between the two friends and frequent visits to each other to discuss the work's progress. This close collaboration continued unabated between the spring and late September of 1901. D'Annunzio was tireless in writing notes and progress reports. He sent Fortuny plans of the stage and stressed the importance of the costumes: 'Amongst the cast, there is an astrologer, a juggler and a Greek slave (from Medieval Greece). The research for these costumes is very important.'[17] It was this research, in fact, that involved Fortuny in his first serious contact with the art of costume.

When D'Annunzio and Eleonora had asked Fortuny to prepare the scenarios of *Francesca da Rimini*, he had accepted with enthusiasm and begun work immediately. He prepared sketches, constructed models using his new system of indirect lighting, designed the costumes and discussed all sorts of details with Gabriele. Fortuny, however, was under the impression that all they wanted from him were sketches and models, whereas D'Annunzio and La Duse expected Mariano to take charge not only of the preliminary plans, but of their realization: the building and painting of the sets, the making of the costumes and the installation of the stage-lighting.

It was at this point that Fortuny began to be plagued by doubts. He realized that he was incapable of taking responsibility for the whole staging of the work; he had neither the organization nor the means for such a large and costly undertaking. D'Annunzio commissioned Masotti, a set designer from Bologna, to go to Venice and help Fortuny to put his ideas into practice. This partnership was not a success, however, and Fortuny wrote to D'Annunzio informing him of his decision not to go ahead with the project, and handing over all his sketches and models. D'Annunzio replied in a magnificently sentimental letter, written in his best poetic style, urging Mariano to change his mind:

> 'Your abandonment has struck me, your brother, more deeply than the betrayal of Paolo Malatesta ... I have composed my tragedy, line by line, with the figures of your art before my eyes. For you I have found beauty so strong and so new that, when you see it, your heart will swell with its power ... I have prepared a world of lines and colours, to which you must give visible and tangible life ... My work – without your collaboration – remains incomplete.'

He also reminded him that 'an artist's promise in the spirit is more solemn and more sacred than any commercial or legal contract'. Besides the plans and dreams that were being destroyed, Fortuny's decision was jeopardizing the vast amounts of money that had been spent on hiring the theatre and assembling the company, which Eleonora was financing. 'Let me convey to you the pain that you are causing me,'[18] D'Annunzio wailed. But Fortuny had made up his mind. Still, the friendship did not break up as a result of Fortuny's decision. On 13 September 1901, nine days after having written to Fortuny, D'Annunzio arrived in Venice accompanied by Eleonora and the three friends were soon discussing theatrical reform and the projected festival theatre on the shores of Lake Albano.

Although the 'ideal' National Theatre was never realized, D'Annunzio's campaign in favour of open theatre was one of the reasons for Palladio's Olympic Theatre in Vicenza being used for a production of *Oedipus Rex* in 1901. The success of this work encouraged the theatre committee to promote similar productions, and they invited D'Annunzio to stage one of his own dramas there. On 28 September D'Annunzio departed for Vicenza, leaving Eleonora in Venice; Fortuny followed him the next day. They studied the theatre and discussed the possibilities of adapting it for one of D'Annunzio's plays, but there were technical difficulties and the plan was never realized. The visit made a great impact on Fortuny, however, and he began seriously to consider the idea of creating a new type of theatrical building.

Soon after his visit to Vicenza, Fortuny returned once more to Paris to continue work on his dome, and by the beginning of 1902 he had produced

First scale model of the cyclorama built in the Palazzo Orfei in 1899. (Museo Fortuny, Venice)

his first large-scale model, which measured five metres in diameter. This early version already incorporated the two features that Fortuny considered essential: it could be folded so as to take up as little space as possible, and it was easily movable. Much of Fortuny's time over the next years was spent trying to perfect these qualities; his final version was installed in La Scala in 1922.

The first full-size model of a mobile, collapsible cyclorama in Mariano's Paris workshop at rue St Charles, 1902. (Museo Fortuny, Venice)

An exhibition of his dome to a small circle of friends in 1902 caused great admiration. Appia, who detested painted scenery and advocated a simplification and abstraction of stage decoration, had found an ally in Fortuny. In an article published in 1904, he wrote: 'Monsieur Mariano Fortuny has invented a completely new system of lighting, based on the properties of reflected lights. The results are extraordinarily successful, and this invention of genius will bring about a radical change in favour of lighting in the stage management of every theatre.'[19]

Appia had his first chance to put his revolutionary ideas into practice

when the Comtesse Martine de Béarn, a frequent visitor to Venice and a great patron of musicians and artists, offered him the job of staging a number of Wagnerian items at the theatre in her *hotel particulier* in Paris. This original project was dropped, but instead Appia prepared a scene from Byron's *Manfred* with music by Schumann, and another from Bizet's *Carmen*. Appia turned to Fortuny for help with the lighting which amazed the audience by its exploitation of hitherto unthought-of possibilities, emphasizing the visual quality of Appia's scenery with its austere architectural character, and creating the right mood of mystery for Byron's work.

There were three performances, on 25, 27 and 28 March 1903, the last night being especially significant since the Comtesse had invited all the most important members of the Parisian theatrical world, from avant-garde artists such as Lugné-Poe to Sarah Bernhardt. The show was a great success, and Appia's ideas were popularized in an article by Count Hermann Keyserling which exercised a direct influence on the performance of *Tristan and Isolde* being prepared by Gustav Mahler and Alfred Roller for the Vienna Opera. This was the first occasion on which Fortuny's new system was used in a large theatre, and Keyserling commented – without mentioning Fortuny by name – that 'part of the lighting system being used was still at the planning stage.'[20]

Appia and Fortuny worked together again in the following year, when Fortuny prepared a model for Act II of *The Valkyrie*, which was never realized. After this they both went their separate ways; Appia continued as a visionary and reformer of the theatre, while the coming years of Fortuny's life were to be devoted to the perfection, diffusion and commercialization of his dome and lighting system.

His friendship with the Comtesse de Béarn, whom he got to know in Venice, was to be a very fruitful one. Martine de Béarn was one of the most important sponsors of music in Paris, along with other eminent ladies such as the Princesse de Polignac, whom Fortuny also knew from Venice, Madame Edouard André and Baroness Rothschild. The Comtesse commissioned Fortuny to reconstruct her theatre, which at that stage was really only a large music room. Mariano naturally installed his dome, which enclosed the whole stage, as well as his system of indirect lighting; he even took it upon himself to make a new curtain. Thus transformed, the theatre reopened on 29 March 1906 with a ballet by Widor, staged by Fortuny, who at last was able to make use of his now fully developed system. It was a magnificent spectacle, and once more the lighting was the star turn. One critic raved: 'it is the canopy of the heavens, the limitless horizon, the air that

Fortuny before the stage of Comtesse de Béarn's private theatre where he installed the first cyclorama, and inaugurated his revolutionary lighting system. He also designed the curtain. 1906. (Museo Fortuny, Venice)

Multi-coloured silk screen first used in the Kroll Theatre, Berlin in 1907. The reflective unit revolved on cylinders and could project every possible shade of colour onto the inner surface of the cyclorama. (Museo Fortuny, Venice)

one breathes, the atmosphere, life.'[21] He concluded by saying that the day would be a milestone in the history of the theatre, using, almost to the word, a phrase that Fortuny himself had used: 'For the first time, on 29 March 1906, theatrical painting has penetrated into the domain of music, that is to say into time.'[22]

Fortuny too was delighted: 'I should like to express my gratitude to the Comtesse Martine de Béarn . . . whose spirit, unique rather than extraordinary, has allowed me to create a stage in the music room of her Parisian house, and to test, on a large scale and under exceptional conditions, my experimental techniques, which I found it difficult, that is to say impossible, to introduce into theatres, where there reigns a mood hostile to any innovation.'[23] The door to success was open, and also the doors to theatres which had previously placed all kinds of obstacles in his path. In May of that year he formed a company, in conjunction with the German electrical firm of A.E.G., to commercialize his dome and his lighting system. Also in the same year the Théâtre de l'Avenue Bosquet became the first public theatre to install his dome – one with a diameter of 12 metres. The following year in collaboration with A.E.G. Fortuny's lighting system, together with a folding dome, was installed in the Theater Kroll in Berlin. There Fortuny met Max Reinhardt, the celebrated German theatre director, who showed great interest in his ideas and in the new system, which he had first admired in Paris in 1905.[24] Using the Spaniard's ideas, Reinhardt decided to make a rigid cyclorama on his own behalf in the Deutsches Theater. Fortuny was most indignant, but it was not to be the only time that his ideas were made use of in this way: years later he remarked, 'this invention has been plagiarized all over the place'.

The dome with the system of lights that A.E.G. was installing in a number of German and Russian theatres represented a great improvement on the earlier models, as it could be either fixed, mobile or foldable.[25] The early rigid dome, constructed of cement over a metal shell, had the advantages of being durable and easy to operate and maintain, but there were also severe drawbacks since it could neither be moved nor folded.

Fortuny regarded the ideal dome as being collapsible, but this called for a completely different construction from the fixed one. The new dome was composed of two layers of opaque cloth in the shape of a quarter sphere mounted on a wire structure; the outer layer was firmly secured to this framework by straps, while the inner layer, the one seen by the audience, hung freely by means of cords. The two layers were kept together by means of a vacuum, which meant that the dome seen by the spectators was completely taut, without any of the folds or wrinkles of the 1902 model. The wire-based framework enabled the dome to be folded in on itself, taking up a minimal space between 1 metre and $1\frac{1}{2}$ metres wide; being mounted on rails, it could be moved backstage whenever it was not needed.

Effects were produced by the light from arc lamps falling on to reflective surfaces made of cloth. Each reflective unit consisted of two pieces of material that revolved on cylinders, in two superimposed circuits. The material of the inner circuit was dyed blue, red and yellow; the outer one was black and white with a hole in the centre, which allowed the light to reach into the inner unit. It was the inner circuit that produced the different colorations, the outer providing the whole range of shades from dark to light. As well as the strips of material there were also coloured panes through which the light shone. This combination of tinted glass and different coloured silk produced every possible shade of colour. Control over the whole mechanism could be exercised from a distance, and only one man was needed to regulate the apparatus, since it was neither heavy nor cumbersome. The system could also be used without the dome, against a conventional backdrop.

The lighting installation consisted of the arc lamps, the device with the coloured surfaces, the ones with the panes of stained glass, the regulator, electric cables and the instruments needed to produce cloud and other effects.

The world of the theatre was not the only one in which Fortuny experimented with the magical properties of light. Using lamps that reflected light against a polished concave surface on the same principle as his theatrical lighting, he succeeded in achieving a diffused light that was perfect for illuminating paintings and other works of art. In 1904 he was commissioned to do the lighting for the exhibition by the Cercle de l'Epatant in Paris, and also, in 1908, the ceilings of the Paris Opéra, which had been painted by Paul Baudry, a friend of his father and his uncle Raymundo.

Now that Fortuny had discovered the world of lighting, stage design and theatre, which offered so many possibilities for his talents, it seemed natural that he would become more deeply involved in it. But this was not to be. He was satisfied with his lighting system and considered that it had reached a certain point of perfection; there was no longer any challenge, and he began to lose interest. So, preferring to leave his ideas in other people's hands for the moment, he left Berlin in December 1907 and returned to Venice.

There he set about finding other challenges in his 'alchemist's attic'. For the alchemist there have never been any barriers: everything has its own validity in the search for the philosopher's stone. The time had come for Fortuny to develop another activity.

CHAPTER

IV

FASHION AND TEXTILES

If for any reason the body must be clothed, the clothing should be to the body as nearly as possible what the body is to the spirit.

HENRY HOLIDAY

In the autobiographical notes he prepared for his American agent Elsie McNeill, Fortuny states that he began to experiment with the printing of textiles in his studio at the Palazzo Orfei in 1907. According to Henri de Régnier, this date should be put forward at least a year.

Fortuny met the Régniers in September 1906 when he invited them to his mother's *palazzo* to see her beautiful collection of textiles. Régnier gives a lengthy account of this visit in *L'Altana ou La Vie Vénitienne, 1899–1924*, which is full of fascinating observations on the idiosyncratic world of Doña Cecilia, María Luisa and Mariano, who was then thirty-five years old. Régnier described him thus:

> 'A Venetian at heart, he loves Venice and knows all the arts inti-
> mately. Like the masters of the Renaissance, he has not restricted
> himself to practising one; his activities have branched out in the
> most diverse directions. At the same time as busying himself with
> bringing new life to stage-lighting, by means of his experiments
> with light, he has revived the dyeing and adorning processes of the
> old weavers and decorators. In the tradition of these men he has
> created some very beautiful materials, both for wall-hangings and
> for clothing, which rival those produced by the craftsmen of the
> past.'[1]

This is the first reference to Fortuny as a creator of textiles.

Fortuny had been familiar with the world of textiles from early child-hood. His father and mother shared a passion for materials, and both of them had visited shops and private houses in Granada, Paris, Morocco and

Fortuny in theatrical costume, c. 1910. (Countess Elsie Lee Gozzi, Venice)

Italy in their search for rare pieces. Part of the collection was sold at auction in 1875, soon after the father's death, but Doña Cecilia retained her own private collection, to which she was constantly adding new pieces. Like everything connected with his father, this world held a special fascination for Fortuny: as a boy he had amused himself by dyeing pieces of material different colours. His own textiles were imbued with the same antique quality possessed by the fabrics, mellowed with age, that had surrounded him as a child. The designs on the velvets, brocades, silks and chasubles in his parents' collection were imprinted upon his imagination many years before he started his own production.

Having succeeded in getting rid of the last tenants from the Palazzo Orfei by the end of 1906, Mariano began to instil into his new home the spirit of the Palazzo Martinengo. Unlike his mother and sister, however, he did not entirely reject the world about him. From his private world in the *palazzo* he remained in touch with all the latest scientific developments in the world outside, tempering his almost monastic life-style with a lively and totally modern spirit of curiosity.

In the early 1900s textiles and fashion played an important part in everyday life. The homes of the middle classes were crammed with fabrics; most of these were in the taste inherited from the preceding generation – the 'Pompous Age', as it has been called – but new styles and designs were

Opposite: Mariano's wife Henriette (right) with a friend, c. 1900. Henriette was a skilled dressmaker who helped produce many of Mariano's models. (Museo Fortuny, Venice)

Scene from a ballet by Ch. M. Widor at the Comtesse de Béarn's house in Paris, 1906. The veils worn by the ballerinas were Fortuny's first textile creations and became known as 'Knossos scarves'. (Museo Fortuny, Venice)

beginning to emerge in tune with the new aesthetic and functional concepts promoted by the reformers of the applied arts. Both literature and painting reflected the importance of textiles. The French poet Baudelaire remarked that 'fabrics speak a mute language, like flowers, like skies, like setting suns'. Painters became interested in fashions and material: each one chose whichever style of dress he preferred for his models, which has left us with a wealth of evidence concerning not only contemporary fashions, but also the way in which people reacted against them. Many artists, either consciously or unconsciously, helped give rise to new fashions through their paintings.

The catalyst that was to enable Fortuny to transform his awareness and appreciation of materials into a creative and tangible form was neither painting nor the new concepts of design, but the theatre. When La Duse and D'Annunzio decided to pass Fortuny's sketches for *Francesca da Rimini* on to Rovescalli, the latter did not alter the costumes, which had already been made, and so the play opened using the wardrobe designed by Fortuny. It would seem though that this first experience was not an unqualified success, since 'the costumes, too meticulously copied by Fortuny from the drawings of Pisanello, hampered the actors' movements'.[2] Yet it must have been for

Below: Model, photographed by Fortuny, showing different ways of draping a Knossos over a pleated and undulated silk gown. (Museo Fortuny, Venice)

him a vital experience, for it had entailed studying in detail not only the different shapes of medieval dress but also the materials.

Although during the years following his work on *Francesca da Rimini* Fortuny was chiefly absorbed in perfecting his dome, the idea of dealing with fabrics and clothes was by then firmly rooted in his mind. It seems likely that the Widor ballet at the Comtesse de Béarn's house in Paris in 1906 involved the first public appearance not only of his lighting system, but also of his first textile creations. A photograph shows the ballerinas wearing his characteristic silk veils, printed with geometric motifs inspired by Cycladic art. These veils with their asymmetical patterns, the result of his first efforts at stamped silk, were made in countless variations by Fortuny up until the 1930s, and were known as 'Knossos scarves'.

It was not by chance that Fortuny chose silk for his first experiments. Silk is an infinitely adaptable fabric whose subtle variations offer a wide range of possibilities. Fortuny's materials were always light and of the highest quality, intended from the start to be not merely ornamental but also worn. The Knossos scarf was, in fact, a type of clothing: it consisted of a rectangular piece of cloth which could be used in a number of different ways, allowing great freedom of expression and movement to the human body. From these

simple scarves, which showed him how to fuse form and fabric, Fortuny developed his entire production of dresses.

For their full effect Knossos scarves needed to be worn as embellishments to a particular type of dress. This dress appeared in around 1907 and was called the 'Delphos robe'. It is undoubtedly Fortuny's most famous creation and eventually became the hallmark of his work, at the expense of the rest of his prolific production. These Delphos robes, which were of pleated silk and very simply cut, hung loosely from the shoulders and were a revolution for the tightly corseted women of 1907. Nearly thirty years later Fortuny painted a portrait of Henriette wearing the robe and the scarf, as if in homage to the muse who had inspired and assisted in the realization of his first *ensemble*.

Scarves that easily adapted themselves to every kind of shape gave Fortuny new ideas, and in his hands were transformed into jackets, tunics or wraps of printed silk. The Delphos robe too inspired other dresses, again of silk, which likewise fell loosely from the shoulders to the ground; sometimes these were gathered in at the waist by a belt, or at the bust in the manner of *Directoire* and Empire dresses.

Shortly after his first work in silk, Fortuny began printing on velvet. He used velvet both as a decorative medium and for dresses. Some of these were similar to his Neo-classical silk dresses, others were medieval or Renaissance style which hung from the shoulders with no belt, reaching down to the ground and generally having a small train at the back. The two pieces of velvet that went into making these dresses were joined at the sides by insets of the same kind of pleated silk as the Delphos robe. Fortuny also used velvet for jackets, capes and cloaks to cover the light Delphos robes and other dresses.

Fortuny trademark registered in Paris on 6 January 1908.

All Fortuny's work in silk and velvet, whether for clothes or for decorative purposes, was basically very simple. From the Delphos robe onwards he made countless variations on his prototypes, but the prototypes themselves did not change or evolve into anything radically different. This makes it almost impossible to establish a chronology of his dresses unless they can be indirectly dated through old photographs or other documents. Fortuny was not interested in fashion *per se*, in constant changes in silhouette, colour, style, skirt-length, collar-shape, fabric and so on. He rejected commercial fashion as understood by the great *couture* houses, with their ornaments, trimmings and unnatural restrictions of the body. Just as Fortuny was a painter who created stage scenery, he was also a painter who created clothes, and not a *couturier*, like Worth, Poiret, Lucille or Coco Chanel. His dresses, his materials, his designs, his concept of clothing were completely divorced from the world of high fashion, and he drew his inspiration from more complex and varied sources. His was an inner world of images, reflecting his own knowledge, experience, and the period in which he lived. And like that era, Fortuny himself had inherited many aspects of the preceding century, including its confusion. It was this confusion that he, as an artist, had to bring to order.

Model photographed by Mariano in a pleated and undulated Delphos with a long silk veil printed in motifs of Cretan inspiration. (Museo Fortuny, Venice)

Fortuny's work as a fabric and dress designer was, like much of his work in other fields, determined by the interaction of external and internal influences. The former were represented by Modernism and the English Aesthetic Movement as well as the presence of a strong Greek element in contemporary art and social *mores*; the latter involved his own character and cultural inheritance. The Arabic and Oriental influence, for example, should be regarded more as an 'internal' factor since it was something that Fortuny inherited from his father.

Painting, both contemporary and classical, particularly Venetian, was one of his main sources of inspiration; he had an extensive and highly personal knowledge of the culture of the past, which enabled him to understand and assimilate Greek, Venetian and exotic elements into his work in a positive way.

His dresses can be related to the reform movements of the period. The exponents of both Modernism and the Aesthetic Movement were aiming for the creation of a modern style freed from the restraints of convention. Dress, they felt, should be artistic, hygienic and functional, and not subject to the whims of fashion which had created a kind of clothing that imprisoned the body like a rigid shell, and was therefore 'ugly'. Followers of the Aesthetic Movement looked back nostalgically to Classical Greek and medieval dress for their models.

During the early 1880s there developed a number of societies dedicated to clothing reforms, which shared the misgivings of the Aesthetes and maintained similar principles to them; they laid particular emphasis on the need for free and rational modes of dress. These societies were supported by Aesthetes and artists alike, but the majority of dress designers at this time were still very much influenced by the prevailing Puritan mentality, and their creations were not nearly as liberated as they were alleged to be, incorporating elements of the contemporary fashions that they were supposed to have rejected. This can be seen in the dresses shown in the first exhibition of the National Health Society in 1882, in which the so-called Greek dresses had more in common with contemporary styles than with their Classical counterparts: they were, in fact, simply variations on the styles of the day. By contrast, the real reformers – the Aesthetes and artists – wanted to create a totally new style of dress, the function of which would be to liberate the body, allow for complete freedom of movement, provide comfort and warmth, and, above all, be beautiful.

It is principally in the paintings and drawings of artists such as Albert Moore, Frederick Leighton, Edward Burne-Jones, Sir Lawrence Alma-Tadema and William Godward that one sees the best evidence of the ideal Aesthetic dress, untainted by the prudishness and moral strictures of the age. Leighton spoke for all of them when he stated that 'by degrees my growing love for form made me intolerant of the restraints and exigencies of costume'.[3] These artists not only rejected the fashion of the day, but also proposed a new fashion in their work, one 'in which no form shall be imposed upon the artist by the tailor'.[4] Taking as their ideals the models of Classical Greece which they felt 'could never be an anachronism',[5] they

'Sapphires' (left) and 'Canaries' (right) by Albert Moore. The shapes and soft colours – pale orange, apricot, salmon – of the artist's imaginary Greek garments were soon to be realized by Fortuny. (By permission of Birmingham Museums and Art Gallery)

revealed a more modern way of dressing than the National Health Society. Their dresses, even if they appeared only in their pictures, were perfectly feasible, like the *chitons* and the *peplos* on the Greek statues they had studied in museums.

With their superior knowledge of the human form, artists were perhaps the most suitable people to design the beautiful 'rational' dress of the Aesthetes. As Walter Crane remarked, 'Regarding dress as a department of design, like design, we may consciously bring to bear upon it the results of artistic experience and knowledge of form.'[6] And the first thing that the study of the human body teaches one is the need to respect it, which is why these painters and sculptors adorned the 'sacred' forms of their models with simple garments, showing, many years before Poiret, that a dress should adapt to the shape of the body without hiding, altering or deforming it.

The fact that the dresses were 'Greek' resulted naturally from these painters' subjects being 'Greek', but often it was the dresses that made the painting 'Greek' in the first place. On the other hand, Greek garments also arose from the Hellenism of the age, which was rapidly taking the place of the Medievalism of the Pre-Raphaelites. In a way, it was a new manifestation of Neo-classicism, and just as David had influenced the dress styles of his era, so these artists influenced the fashions of *fin-de-siècle* Europe.

Because these English painters lived in an environment that was very concerned with the reform of clothing, their 'Greek' dresses were more realistic than those of similar European painters, as though they were aware, when producing their pictures, that their contemporaries might wish to wear them. In the paintings of Moore and Leighton, the dresses not only remind one of Fortuny's Delphos because of their Greek inspiration and their fine pleating but also because of their ambiguous colours – whites, soft yellows, Malta orange, golden or pale pinks – in which light played an important role. Occasionally an 'ideal' dress would actually be produced, as in the case of Alma-Tadema. It is not without reason that Alma-Tadema has been called the painter of 'Victorians in Togas'; 'satin dresses made by Liberty's of London "*à la* Tadema" were very popular and wealthy American women idled about in "Tadema Togas".'[7]

There were a number of similarities between Alma-Tadema and Fortuny. Alma-Tadema also developed into a multi-faceted artist, but not by adhering to the tenets of the Aesthetic Movement; he achieved it, like Fortuny, in a completely personal way as a result of a highly inquisitive mind and a strong desire to do everything himself. In an attempt to recreate Classical subjects archaeologically, he carefully studied the art of that era

'Silver Favourites' by Sir Lawrence Alma-Tadema, 1903. The pleated dresses and veils of these maidens bear a striking resemblance to Fortuny's Delphos and Knossos. (City of Manchester Art Galleries)

and, again like Fortuny, assembled a vast photographic library containing no less than one hundred and sixty-eight volumes.

When Alma-Tadema died in 1912, Fortuny was already forty-one years old and had been working on his fabrics and clothes for a number of years, but artists like Godward and Wontner continued to portray girls in Classical dress in paintings that bore a strong resemblance to the portrait of Henriette in the Delphos *ensemble* shown on page 179.

The reformists, whose ideas were rarely covered in the influential newspapers and magazines, could not gain access to the public at large. In an effort to overcome this they created their own means of communication – publications such as *Aglaia* (an ancient Greek word meaning 'beauty'), in which Walter Crane and Henry Holiday collaborated, and the *Rational Dress Gazette* – but the readership was composed of intellectuals and other progressives who were already familiar with their propositions. The reformists possessed neither the means of manufacturing dresses nor the wherewithal to promote them. When an artist created a dress, it was for his wife, his girlfriend or his models. In many instances these were the designers or 'publicists' of the dresses, women such as Jane Morris, Joanna Hefferman, who was Whistler's 'White Girl', Lady Windsor, whose portrait Burne-Jones painted, Ellen Terry, or the members of the Rational Dress Society.

Liberty's opened their first shop in 1875 for the import and sale of oriental goods from Japan, China, India and Persia. It proved a great success

'Green Beads' by William Clarke Wontner, 1916. Painters like Wontner continued to paint in the Neo-classical tradition of the Victorian painters long after Fortuny began producing his dresses and fabrics. (Courtesy of Sotheby Parke Bernet)

with the Aesthetes, who in turn influenced the designs that Liberty's were beginning to produce in England. Soon Indian silks began to be printed with their own designs – the famous Liberty Art Silks. Oriental silks were particularly popular with artists, 'because they could get nothing of European make that would drape properly, and was of sufficiently well-balanced colouring to satisfy their eye'.[8] This illustrates how their interest in fabric and costume was not restricted merely to their paintings.

A few shops, like Liberty's and the Aesthetic Gallery, were channels for the diffusion of the new ideas, but most of their 'artistic' dresses were just a mixture of Aesthetic elements and contemporary fashion. Nevertheless, as Walter Crane remarked, 'Whatever vulgarity, absurdity and insincerity might have been mixed up by its enemies with what was to be known as the aesthetic movement, it undoubtedly did indicate a general desire for greater beauty in ordinary life and gave us many charming materials and colours which, in combination with genuine taste, produced some very beautiful as well as simple dresses.'[9]

This new feeling about dress was to be continued by the Modernist Movement or Art Nouveau, which followed Aestheticism, as shown by the dresses of Van de Velde, Margarete von Braunitsch or the Viennese Secession designers and artists like Klimt and Moser. However, the dresses of these designers lost the purity and simplicity of the Aesthetic artists, as they incorporated all the complicated motifs and decorative elements of Art Nouveau. Symbolists and Decadents found inspiration for the dresses of their mysterious figures in the East, the Middle Ages, the Renaissance or Velazquez.

Theatre played an important role in fashion. In dramatic fiction, as in pictorial fiction, dresses could be designed with fantasy, which had a strong influence on a public acclimatized by the Symbolists to images that had no place in everyday reality. Artistic dress, which differed from the predominant fashion, also possessed a theatrical and escapist look, like a sort of mask. In this sense, Aesthetic, artistic and rational dress all had the same magical ability to transport their wearer beyond the realms of reality, a reality that had to be modified and was dominated by a whole series of social and economic pressures and prejudices. To a certain extent, dress had assumed the power of great art.

In the first decade of the twentieth century the Classical spirit transcended painting and art to influence social life. As Lady Cooper exclaimed, 'Greek – everything must be Greek.'[10] But whereas Neo-classicism had maintained a complete dominance, as in the case of fashion, the Greek spirit

Emilie Flöge by Gustav Klimt. The Modernist Movement, which followed Aestheticism, maintained the new feeling for dress but incorporated more complicated motifs and decorative elements. (With permission of Galerie Welz, Salzburg)

Above: Fortuny's silhouetted figures in wood for displaying clothes. The models are draped in Knossos veils with Cretan and Coptic motifs. Artist's photograph. (Museo Fortuny, Venice)

Right: Fortuny regarded his concept of dress as an invention, registering it in Paris in 1909. The accompanying diagrams were included in the patent. (Office National de la Propriété Industrielle, Lyon)

of these years shared its dominance with many other influences, like Orientalism, with which it generally became intermingled.

Isadora Duncan revived Greek dance in her own personal way. She toured Europe showing her dances, and everywhere was enthusiastically acclaimed. With Isadora 'there reappeared those free, natural movements that correspond either to the dancer's instinctive imagination or to the expression of her feelings and her thoughts.'[11] This new repertoire of movements was a paean of praise to the plasticity and beauty of the human body, and it was for this reason that Isadora began her reform by rejecting the classical uniform of the ballerina, the tutu, for a dress that would mould

itself to the body. Adopting the ancient tunic that Leighton and Moore proposed, she showed that costume could affect the development of dance, because 'the history of ballet is closely linked to the guises of ballet, in other words with dress'.[12] Her free and highly individual form of dance, so different from classical ballet which – until the advent of the *Ballets Russes* – was cold and subject to a mechanical discipline, opened the doors to modern ballet as understood by Martha Graham or Doris Humphrey.

This whole mood, this feeling for a new type of garment beyond the realms of fashion, which hung from the shoulders and allowed for complete freedom of movement, glorifying the human form like the clothes of ancient

Greece, and which was stimulated by painting, dance and theatre and by artistic women, prepared the way for Fortuny's work.

Fortuny was surely informed of all the latest developments, thanks to his constant travels to France, and probably also England, and his contacts with the theatre, with artists, *literati* and society patrons. In addition, Alma-Tadema, Leighton, Watts, Burne-Jones and Walter Crane had all exhibited paintings in the Biennale in Venice.

The artistic dress, the rational dress, the functional dress, the medieval dress and the Utopian dress of the theorists and artists alike, were to become reality in Fortuny's hands. It was he who created that simple, unrestricting, hygienic and beautiful dress, subject to neither fashions nor changes, which had been sought by everybody. In addition, he succeeded in ensuring that he would be frustrated by neither fashion nor convention.

Fortuny regarded his new concept of dress as an invention, and even patented it in the *Office National de la Propriété Industrielle* in Paris on 4 November 1909.[13] It is interesting to note the language he used to describe his invention; certainly a very original and modern way of talking about a dress.

'This invention is related to a type of garment derived from the Classical robe, but its design is so shaped and arranged that it can be worn and adjusted with ease and comfort.

'... A garment whose invention consists of a sheath, open at the top and bottom, whose width can be equal to its length, widening or narrowing from top to bottom or at varying points, according to the general appearance and look which it is desired to give to the garment. The material can be smooth or pleated, this detail being independent of the invention.

'At the top the sheath is laid flat so that the two edges are placed side by side, and these two edges are brought together and fastened at points *d* and *e* in a manner to be decided upon: an opening *a* placed in the centre and forming the neckline, two side openings *c c* designed for the arms to go through and two intermediary openings *b b* whose edges are laced together. Between points *e* and points *g* at the sides ribbons are threaded obliquely so that one can adjust and modify the distance *r* which determines the bottom of the sleeve according to the height and measurements of the wearer. These laces are placed for preference inside the garment so as to be invisible.'

This dress, executed in pleated silk, was the Delphos. Unlike the recon-

The Charioteer of Delphos, 475–70 B.C., the bronze statue which gave its name to Fortuny's most famous dress.

structions of Alma-Tadema, the Delphos was a modern and original creation. It gained its name from the bronze statue of the Delphic *Charioteer*, but the folds of the latter's tunic are too broad to do anything more than suggest the countless fine pleats of the Delphos. Truer models can be found on the archaic *korai* sculptures dating from the sixth century BC. During that period dress was so important to sculptors that the evolution of the *korai*, that is to say of art, can be better understood in terms of the treatment of the folds than of the figures' anatomy. Fortuny kept numerous illustrations of these sculptures in his photographic archive.

There were different types of garment, but the one favoured by these Greek sculptors was the Ionic *chiton*. The dress hung in folds and was gathered in by a belt which was itself covered by the fold (or *kolpos*) it created. A short mantle called a *himation* was sometimes fastened over the right shoulder, passing beneath the left arm. This resulted in one side falling lower than the other, producing an asymmetrical effect. The *himation* was in fact the forerunner of the Delphos overblouse.

In general terms, the Delphos was made in the same way as the *chiton*, being sewn in a cylindrical shape with holes for the head and arms, but with the great difference that the material was silk, and not wool or linen like the Greeks used, and was also pre-pleated. The cut was simple, consisting of a long gown suspended from the shoulders and clinging to the body, three or four widths of material being used for each dress.

The model originally described in Fortuny's patent was a Delphos with batwing sleeves, but numerous variations were subsequently produced, some with short sleeves, some with long, wide sleeves tied at the wrist, and others that were sleeveless. This last version was probably a later model created in the late 1920s. As a rule, the dresses had wide, 'bateau' necks. Some were more closed and others could be V-shaped, but they always had a cord that allowed one to adjust them to the shoulders. There was a silk belt printed with geometric and foliar decorations which could be used or not, according to individual preference. All the dresses reached to the floor, and Fortuny himself preferred them to cover the feet, as they do in his own photographs.

The overblouse was always sewn to the simple Delphos and was of the same pleated silk and the same colour, forming an integral part of it. Its ends were irregular, with two long ends generally at the side, tapering to a point. In some cases it tapered to four points, one at each side, one at the front and one at the back, as in the Cecil Beaton photograph on page 206. The border of the dress, its overblouse, sides and cuffs were usually finished with a series

Opposite: Silk velvet cloak over a blue and grey silk satin Delphos. (Liselotte Höhs, Venice/E. Momeñe). Set against a velvet fabric with motifs of Renaissance inspiration. (Museo Fortuny, Venice/E. Momeñe)

of small Venetian glass beads in different colours. These had a dual function: they were ornamental and they also weighted the dress down, ensuring that it did not 'float' but clung to the contours of the body. These beads were a typically Venetian product, and Fortuny was a great lover and collector of Venetian glass.

It is still a mystery how the pleats of the Delphos were achieved, and although he patented the process in 1909[14] there remains much conjecture about it. The method needed a lot of manual work, since the folds are all different and irregular. They were probably put into the material when it was wet, perhaps still under water, with heat being applied later to ensure that they remained permanent. During the latter process it is possible that a piece of thread may have been passed through each group of pleats in order to tighten them for a time.

The patent included a means of undulating the material horizontally once it had been pleated. To undulate the silk he designed a system of horizontally placed copper or porcelain tubes that could be heated from within. The pleated piece of silk, still wet, would be placed between these

Opposite:
Model photographed by Fortuny in four different designs. Top left: Tunic of silk gauze trimmed with Venetian glass beads. Top right: Short cape of Venetian influence: silk gauze with a lace design, trimmed with glass beads. Bottom left: Silk gown printed with a Persian motif. Bottom right: Early version of Delphos photographed in the Palazzo Orfei against a background of printed velvet. (Museo Fortuny, Venice)

Below: Diagram showing method of printing fabric with roller stencils, patented in 1910. Fortuny's system was a forerunner of the modern rotary screen-printing machine. (Office National de la Propriété Industrielle, Lyon)

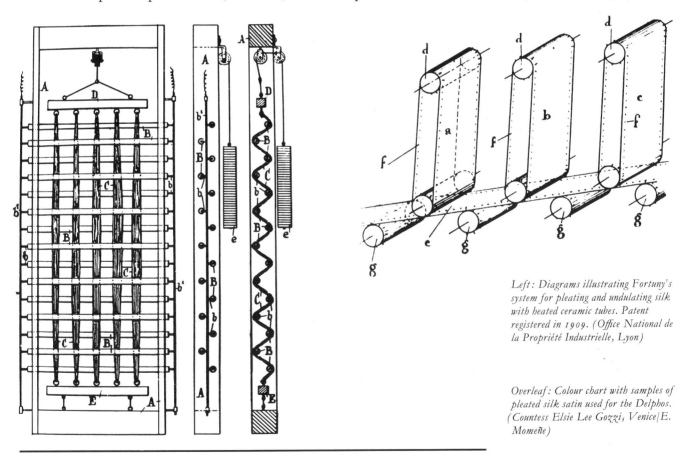

Left: Diagrams illustrating Fortuny's system for pleating and undulating silk with heated ceramic tubes. Patent registered in 1909. (Office National de la Propriété Industrielle, Lyon)

Overleaf: Colour chart with samples of pleated silk satin used for the Delphos. (Countess Elsie Lee Gozzi, Venice/E. Momeñe)

tubes and the permanently undulating effect created by the heat.

Fortuny's techniques were simple but very effective. Today there are Delphos dresses over forty years old whose pleats are still as tight and crisp as when they were new. The best way to keep the pleats is to store the dresses rolled, twisting them tightly from both ends into a ball. This makes them very convenient for travelling: they need little space for packing, and there is no need of ironing. One has only to unroll the dresses and wear them.

Before being made up, the silks were dyed every colour imaginable. The soft, gentle shades favoured by the Aesthetes predominated, but in Fortuny's hands they gained a special richness and brilliance. The silk was dipped several times, each application enriching the colour which, due to the transparency of the dye, possessed an ambiguous and living quality that made it change according to light and movement. This magical effect could only be achieved by relentless hard work and experimentation.

Henriette, for her part, was Fortuny's assistant as well as his muse. She was extraordinarily good with her hands and her skills as a seamstress made her the perfect person to bring Mariano's ideas to life. She also shared his taste for the Greek and the exotic, generally wearing her hair in the Greek fashion.

Apart from the Classical influence, there were two sources of inspiration for Fortuny's dresses and textiles: historical eras like the Renaissance and sixteenth-century Venetian art, and the world of the East.

The masters of the Renaissance and the great painters of Venice re-

Overleaf.
Top left: Short coat of silk velvet
stencilled in gold. (The Phoenix,
Museum, Arizona/E. Momeñe)
Top right: Theatrical costume for a
production of Othello in 1935, draped
over a Delphos. (Liselotte Höhs,
Venice/E. Momeñe) Bottom left:
Cape with hood: silk velvet printed with
a late 15th century Venetian style
motif. (Tina Chow, New York/E.
Momeñe) Bottom right: The Delphos
silk belts were stencilled in gold or
silver. The mantle lining, mostly in silk,
was considered part of the outfit and
carefully matched for colour. (Countess
Elsie Lee Gozzi, Venice/E. Momeñe)
Far right: Detail of Delphos pleats
beneath a silk velvet coat stencilled in
gold with motifs reinterpreting Coptic
and Cretan designs. (Countess Elsie Lee
Gozzi, Venice/E. Momeñe)

vealed to him the rich designs and colours of the costumes and fabrics of those ages. Everywhere in Venice there were reminders of this past glory. In every church there was a Tintoretto, a Bellini or a Carpaccio to recall that bygone era in which fabrics had played such an important part. At that time, Venice was one of the great centres of the European textile industry, and her velvets, brocades and damasks were famous throughout the world. Situated between East and West, she incorporated into her fabrics the luxury, the quality and the designs of an exotic world that fascinated Fortuny, as it had also fascinated his father and his mother. The paintings of Masaccio, Botticelli and Titian provided ideas for shapes, colours and motifs, many of which originated in China, Persia or Turkey. Fortuny would reinterpret them, producing luxurious yet simply cut velvet jackets, wraps, mantles and capes.

It was perhaps Carpaccio, one of Fortuny's favourite artists, who inspired him most. In *A la Recherche du Temps Perdu* Proust, speaking through the narrator, remarks that this 'genial son of Venice'[15] had taken the idea for one of his velvet capes 'from the shoulder of a companion of *La Calza* (a figure in one of Carpaccio's paintings: the *Miracle of the Relic of the Cross*), to hang it over the shoulders of so many Parisian women.'[16]

Eastern and Islamic cultures were another important source of Fortuny's inspiration: the Japanese kimono, the Coptic tunic, the Arabic abaias, the North African burnous, the Oriental caftan, the Moroccan djellabah, the Turkish dolman, the jubbah and the Indian sari were all developed by him in an original way. He also produced ecclesiastical garments that recall the richness and quality of medieval chasubles.

All the dresses were produced in the studio at the Palazzo Orfei like true works of art. They were made by hand, individually, as were all the materials that went into them: the pleated and printed silk, the velvets, the cords that were used to gather them or unite the different parts, the linings which were of satin or sometimes, for greater warmth, of silk, wool or synthetic fibres, the belts and even the labels. Except for the glass beads ordered from the Murano glass factory, everything was made on the premises, including accessories; as the dresses had no pockets their wearers needed bags, which Fortuny made from his own multi-coloured velvet in very simple designs. The veils, foulards and shawls were also designed, dyed and printed in the *palazzo*.

Although the number of prototypes he designed was quite small, every dress, like every piece of material, was different. Each creation was in a sense unique and deserving of his special attention, and he never lost this attitude

Opposite: Carpaccio's Miracle of the Relic of the True Cross *(1494–5). The cape on the foreground figure seen also in Fortuny's copy on p. 52 was mentioned by Proust as the inspiration for Mariano's velvet cloaks. (Accademia, Venice)*

Overleaf:
Left: Detail of Delphos showing sleeve and Venetian beading. (Tina Chow, New York/E. Momeñe)

Right: Ivory Delphos with short tunic and batwing sleeves. (Countess Elsie Lee Gozzi, Venice/E. Momeñe)

Below: Long gown of pale silver-green velvet with a Renaissance style pattern in muted blue and gilded metal with pleated silk insets at the sides and sleeves. Sold at auction, November 1979. (Christie's East, New York)

even when with the passing of the years the small workshop grew into a full-scale manufacturing business.

For his textile production Fortuny designed thousands of patterns throughout his life, often printing the same ones again in different colour combinations. From the Renaissance one of his favourite designs was the open pomegranate, which originated from the Chinese lotus flower; Mariano was to print this in several variations. He used many other fifteenth-century vegetable motifs that came to Europe from Persia and Turkey. Lucca motifs he used frequently in his panelled velvet dresses with silk pleats at the sides. Further sources for his designs were the European textiles of the seventeenth, eighteenth and nineteenth centuries, as well as many motifs from Cretan, Arabic (epigraphic textiles), Indian, Chinese, Japanese and later pre-Colombian and Oceanic (Maori) art. Fortuny did not merely copy old designs, but reinterpreted them, like his dresses. In addition he created his own original designs. He also experimented with photography, producing some very interesting and advanced patterns, but to judge by what has survived, few were ever printed.

Like his parents, Mariano had a large personal collection of textiles which he looked after with great care. It was constantly referred to, and taught him a great deal, especially about colour, texture and feeling. Printing was the only technique he used for achieving his remarkable effects: the quality of the old velvets, the brocades enriched with silver and gold, the damasks and even complicated textiles such as the 'zetonino velluto ad inferriata', a Venetian speciality.

Working like an artisan and researching like an alchemist, Fortuny perfected his dyeing and printing techniques, experimenting with all kinds of materials including linen, wool and others. But above all he preferred silk and velvet, the oldest and most luxurious fabrics. Silk he used in all its different varieties – crêpes, satins, gauzes, muslins and voiles – which he imported directly from China and Japan. The velvet was a very light silk velvet usually imported from France, but possibly also from England and Italy as well. He bought it, like the silk, in a raw state which was white or slightly creamy.

The whole process from raw materials to the final result depended on Fortuny. Not only were the different printing techniques his: he would also produce the dyes, the colours, the blocks or stencils, and the machines. To begin with he employed one of the simplest processes using wooden blocks, some of which are still kept at the Palazzo Fortuny. This was the technique he used to print the first Knossos. His early attempts at printing were on raw or very lightly dyed material, but he soon realized the importance of the

foundation colour. Using vegetable-based colours he produced dyes in which he submerged his cloth successively, layer upon layer, in order to produce those rich, mellow colours whose transparency resembled that of the tempera paints he used on his canvases. On the cloth thus prepared he would use his wood-blocks, creating all kinds of harmonies and rhythms in different colours. Soon he improved this method with an original invention patented in 1909.[17] This consisted of first printing with an engraved block prepared with an especially absorbent product which followed the lines of the drawing. On the same fabric he would apply different colours with other blocks, not necessarily corresponding to the lines of the drawing; by capillary action these colours would extend to the outlines of the original drawing. Since there was no need to have a perfectly engraved block for each colour, this process was both quicker and cheaper.

In order to achieve new colour effects for a wider range of designs, he combined this system with stencils and hand-painting. Stencils had been developed to a high standard of quality and perfection by the Japanese, and these *katagami*[18] had had a great influence on European design during the second part of the nineteenth century. Fortuny was well acquainted with Japanese designs and techniques – not only did he possess books on the subject, he also had a collection of *katagami*. In Europe at this time metal stencil plates or *pochoirs* were used, and many of Fortuny's designs were made in this way. But in order for these experiments and early attempts to be turned into a professional high-quality product, the artisan techniques had to be altered.

In 1910 he patented a radical improvement of this technique, the patent being granted in the following year.[19] He was unconvinced by the mechanical systems invented during the nineteenth century; engraved roller printing, for example, seemed to him too expensive and too limiting. The use of stencils, on the other hand, had a number of advantages as regards cost and quality and also ease of transfer of the design onto the material, and he set about improving the process: his aim was 'to increase and also give continuity to the surface of the stencils, which are limited at the moment.'[20] The stencils that Fortuny proposed were made of very fine cloth such as silk, and similar to ones which had already been used at Lyons around the middle of the nineteenth century.

The silk was soaked in gelatine, on top of which the design was outlined by means of a chemical solution, a process that could be done either manually or photographically. When the treated material was exposed to the light, the areas of gelatine covered with the chemical solution became

Above: Machinery designed by Fortuny for the production of his textiles. (Museo Fortuny, Venice)

Overleaf:
Left: Velvet fabric printed with Renaissance style motif. (Liselotte Höhs, Venice)
Right: Silk velvet fabric printed in a motif of Turkish influence. (Liselotte Höhs, Venice)
Box, top right: Ecclesiastical vestment with Renaissance motif.
Box, bottom right: Velvet cape with hood, Venetian Renaissance motif. The hood is lined with velvet with a second Renaissance motif. (Museo Fortuny, Venice/E. Momeñe)

Opposite:
Top left: Carnavalet: 17th century style pattern named after the Paris Museum for which it was first made.
Top right: Fragonard: 18th century French Toile style pattern, named after the painter.
Bottom left: Moresco: An early Moorish style design.
Bottom right: Granada: Modern Spanish design named after Fortuny's birthplace.
(Countess Elsie Lee Gozzi, Venice)

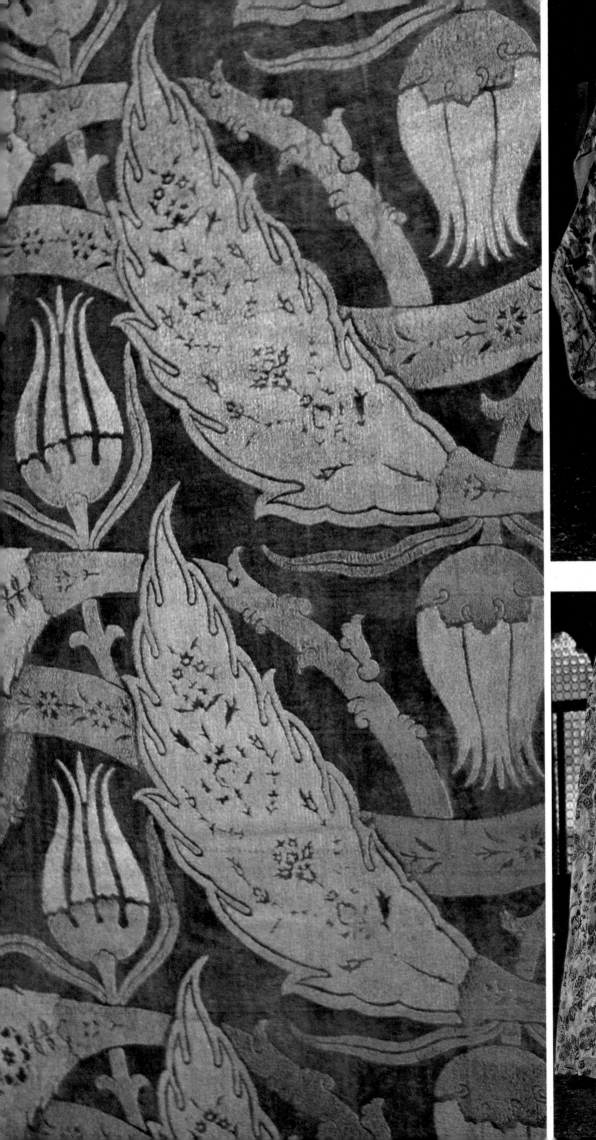

insoluble. The remainder disappeared with washing, leaving behind the design that was to be reproduced. The stencil prints obtained in this way lent themselves to a rotational system of reproduction, capable of producing a greater quantity of cloth with no lessening of the quality. This system is, in fact, the forerunner of the modern rotary screen-printing machine.

To achieve the particular crinkled or flaky effects of his velvets he probably applied the pigments over a natural paste such as albumin, pressing the colours into the material with a roller or other specially designed tool; this produced a rough texture on the printed areas. He often used this method to apply the gold or silver-like powder with which he added further richness to the different colour combinations. Very often the pieces would be re-touched in tempera by brush to enhance the effect.

The process was continually being improved, but the quality of the end product – his unique and highly individualistic fabrics – depended not on mechanical ingenuity but on Fortuny's artistic sense. He conceived his textiles as if they were paintings, and treated them as such. He never used the same design or identical colour combination in any two pieces of fabric. Even in a single piece the colour constantly changes with the light, one layer appearing through another so that no two areas are alike. Thus Proust speaks of a particular velvet as being 'of an intense blue which, as my gaze extended over it, was changed into a malleable gold, by those same transmutations which, before the advancing gondolas, change into flaming metal the azure of the Grand Canal.'[21] As many as fifteen to eighteen different colours might be used in the same piece. He never used the chemical colours that could be found everywhere; when almost nobody produced or used natural colours, he made his own. He imported all the different ingredients – the cochineal (a small insect that produces a red tint) from Mexico, indigo from India, and other plants and herbs from Brazil. In his laboratory he would reduce these ingredients to powder and mix them to obtain the magical and unique colours with which he reinterpreted the old techniques.

Fortuny invented fashion outside fashion, fashion that does not change, fashion as art. It is hard to imagine a woman today wearing a Poiret, a Paquin or a Patou. Dresses by these well-known designers and fashion innovators are marked by the stigma of fashion: they were created with the notion that they would not be used the following season or the following year, when they would in any case have lost their magic. Fortuny's, by contrast, are timeless clothes. Their beauty lies in the elegant simplicity, the perfect cut, the quality of the material and the sensuality of the colours. All these elements, perfectly integrated, make a Fortuny garment a work of art.

Overleaf:
Top left: Cotton satin with motif in gold metal inspired by Islamic art.
Top right: Cotton satin with Orfeo motif in silver metal.
Bottom left: Cotton with a motif inspired by Polynesian textiles.
Bottom right: Cotton twill with geometrical motif.
(Liselotte Höhs, Venice/E. Momeñe)

Opposite: Display of Fortuny garments and textiles in the salon-studio on the first floor of the Palazzo Orfei.
(Countess Elsie Lee Gozzi, Venice)

FORTUNY AND THE WORLD

*Of all the indoor and outdoor gowns that Mme de Guermantes wore,
those which seemed most to respond to a definite intention, to be endowed
with a special significance, were the garments made by Fortuny from
old Venetian models. Is it their historical character, is it rather the fact
that each one of them is unique that gives them so special a significance
that the pose of the woman who is wearing one while she waits for you
to appear or while she talks to you assumes an exceptional importance...?*

MARCEL PROUST

*Mariano seated with his mother in the
Palazzo Orfei. (Countess Elsie Lee
Gozzi, Venice)*

Fortuny's family had left him with enough money to live comfortably and
conduct his affairs in a manner that suited his temperament. His driving
force was the desire to remain independent. Once his enthusiasm had been
fired by a medium which did not result in individual works of art that hung
on walls, but rather ones that hung from women's shoulders, he had to
discover a way of reaching his audience. After his experience with A.E.G.,
which had undertaken the production of his dome and then introduced
various modifications and innovations of their own, he dreaded becoming
involved with a large company that would force him to work to its requirements. As a result, he decided to market his dresses and materials himself.
There was a considerable risk involved in placing oneself outside the
fashion world, however, since it represented a vast commercial network
which controlled everything to do with clothes. Then as now, it was nearly
impossible to reach the public without its help, an obstacle that had proved
the undoing of dress reformers before Fortuny.

At the turn of the century, the *couturiers* of the great fashion houses
ran a system according to a rigid set of requirements. Rational and Aesthetic
dress, by breaking the rules, naturally threatened this system. Just as every
establishment invariably rejects its rebels or assimilates them in a way that
deprives them of their power, so the fashion world first ignored the Aesthetes
and then incorporated their reforms after modifying them. Having dispos-
sessed the dresses of their essentially revolutionary quality, they turned
them into something superficial – that is to say, something fashionable.

This powerlessness in the face of high fashion, suffered by reformers

Left: Illustration from a 1924 issue of French Vogue: a velvet gown with pleated silk insets, a silk coat and a cushion. (© The Condé Nast Publications Ltd.)

Opposite: Colette Alliot-Lugaz in a Delphos and velvet mantle stencilled in silver and gold, with a motif inspired by Cretan art. The surround shows a detail of the pleated silk fabric in a Delphos gown. (Countess Elsie Lee Gozzi, Venice/Gerard Amsellem)

Frontispiece designed by Adolfo de Carolis for the book Notturno *by Mariano's friend Gabriele D'Annunzio.*

Opposite: Lee MacPherson, author of several 1920s Broadway successes, wearing a white Delphos for the opening night of her King of Nowhere. *(Christie's, London/A. C. Cooper Ltd.)*

and artists alike, Fortuny resolved in his own way. If his creations had little to do with the fashion of the day, neither did his method of production or distribution. Everything, from the printing of the cloth to the selling of the finished dress, was under his personal control. The entire operation was initially organized around the Palazzo Orfei: it was there that the materials were sent, and there that they were printed, cut and sewn. A shop was set up on the ground floor where some of the first dresses and fabrics were sold to the public. As the demand for them grew, Fortuny gradually created a small international network of shops and carefully selected agents, but he never produced in great quantities and his sales and distribution system remained simple as he preferred to oversee it himself.

The early publicity for Mariano's work was achieved by quiet, subtle methods, in sharp contrast to the outrageous and often splendid ways of Paul Poiret – the most important *couturier* of the time – who paraded through Longchamps with models wearing his extravagant creations, and organized grandiose parties to promote his latest ideas. High fashion had been evolving at its own slow pace, and when Poiret finally arrived on the scene the magazines proudly proclaimed the new fashion clothes as if they had just been conceived: 'We are at present enjoying not only the most salutary but the most artistic style since the Greek era, in which we are neither sloping nor square but just natural graceful things.'[1] Typically, the fashion establishment and its designers were now adopting as their own a concept that they had rejected twenty years earlier when it was first presented by their opponents.

No artist or designer had been able to produce and market a viable model on his own. Why then did Fortuny succeed where others had failed? The answer must lie partially in the artist's own strength of character, his enormous self-confidence and the undeniable quality of his products. By 1911, when his fashions and textiles appeared in an exhibition of decorative art at the Louvre, his fame had already been firmly established. Nevertheless, a large part of his success can be attributed to the small group of admirers initially attracted to his creations; writers like D'Annunzio and Proust, entertainers like Eleonora Duse and Isadora Duncan, and influential figures such as Queen Marie of Rumania. These luminaries and socialites created a vital link between the solitary worker in Venice and the people in the great cities of Europe and America.

D'Annunzio was undoubtedly among the first to become familiar with Fortuny's dresses. In 1908 he started work on a novel entitled *Forse che sì, Forse che no (Maybe yes, Maybe no)* which he published two years later. The

heroine is dressed in the following manner:

> 'She was wrapped in one of those very long scarves of Oriental gauze that the alchemist dyer Mariano Fortuny steeps in the mysterious recesses of his vats, which are stirred with a wooden spear, now by a sylph, now by a hobgoblin, and he draws them out coloured with strange, dream-like shades, and then he prints on them with a thousand blows of his burnishing tool new generations of stars, plants and animals. Surely with Isabella Inghirani's scarf he must have suffused the dye with a small amount of the pink stolen by his sylph from a rising moon.'[2]

The writer's imaginative description of Fortuny's Knossos scarf may well have been based directly on the woman who had inspired the character: the Marchesa Casati. He had met her in Milan around 1906, but La Casati, as she was better known, actually lived in Venice not far from Doña Cecilia's *palazzo* on the Grand Canal. D'Annunzio used to say that she was the only woman who had ever surprised him; always extravagantly made up, she was addicted to magic and necromancy, and lived surrounded by animals. Visitors to her home – as Isadora Duncan discovered – would find themselves face to face with bulldogs, parrots, snakes, gorillas, orangutans and leopards, all of which the Marchesa took for walks in her garden and occasionally even in St Mark's Square.

In the years leading up to the First World War, her house was frequently the scene of magnificent parties, to which Fortuny was always invited, and she became notorious for welcoming guests in outlandish costumes, surrounded by her mascots and black servants bearing flaming torches. La Casati liked Mariano's clothes above all for their shock appeal and was especially attracted to his velvet capes and mantles whose theatrical, somewhat ornamental quality prefigured the visions of the *Ballets Russes*. Yet his creations were not meant for masquerade balls, and she eventually abandoned them for more outrageous attire of her own design.

From the start Fortuny's dresses appealed to women of a certain refinement and discrimination. Lady Diana Cooper recalls in the first volume of her memoirs, *The Rainbow Comes and Goes*, how as early as 1907 'Princess Murat, a fascinating surprise and totally different from anything we knew ... wore the first of these tanagra-esque garments, later sold by thousands (many to me over twenty years) made by Fortuny of Venice – timeless dresses of pure thin silk cut severely straight from shoulder to toe, and kept wrung like a skein of wool. In every crude and subtle colour, they clung like mermaid's scales.'[3]

The interior of the Palazzo Orfei, now the Palazzo Fortuny, as it appears today:
Glass cases (above) containing busts of Mariano's father and himself as a child, by Gemito, as well as a bust of his grandfather, Federico de Madrazo. The painting and the metal desk lamp are both by Fortuny.
Four small portraits of Henriette and one of Fortuny in later years (below) hang beside his large painting of María Luisa (shown on p. 34). The curtains, wall, and cushions are all covered in his fabrics. In the foreground is a lampshade of his own design.

Marcel Proust. The author was fascinated by Fortuny and his dresses, and made numerous references to both throughout Remembrance of Things Past. *(Radio Times Hulton Picture Library)*

Parisian high society, including the ladies from the ancient families of the Faubourg St Germain, soon became aware of Fortuny's creations and longed to possess them. Elaine de Greffulhe, who was then Comtesse de Guiche and later Duchesse de Gramont, had several which are now in the Musée de la Mode et du Costume in Paris. She herself may have been introduced to the dresses by her mother, the famous Comtesse de Greffulhe, who served as a model for the character of the Duchesse de Guermantes in

Proust's *Remembrance of Things Past*.

These influential women of the *beau monde*, whose lives Proust was to describe in such minute detail, certainly made him aware of Fortuny. On at least sixteen occasions throughout his novel there are references to Fortuny or to his dresses. In the volume entitled *The Captive*, Fortuny constitutes a whole *leitmotiv*. While he serves a definite literary function in the book and does not exist independently of the main theme (that of Albertine), Fortuny is the only character in the whole of Proust's long work who retains a real-life name and identity. The descriptions, comments and associations go far beyond the needs of literature, reflecting a very real knowledge of and fascination for his dresses.

Proust had an additional reason for being familiar with Fortuny's work and perhaps with the artist himself, although there is no definite evidence to confirm their meeting. In 1894 Proust was introduced to Reynaldo Hahn and from that moment on the two became best of friends, seeing each other often, even towards the end of the author's life when he hardly left his bedroom and worked feverishly through the night to complete his masterpiece. Reynaldo's sister, Maria, married Mariano's uncle, Raymundo de Madrazo, in 1899. Raymundo, Coco and the latter's young stepmother, Maria, frequently visited the Fortuny family, dividing their time between the Palazzo Martinengo and the Palazzo Orfei, where they admiringly followed Mariano's progress. In 1916 Proust, forever obsessed with detail, wrote to Maria from the Boulevard Haussman with a series of questions: 'Do you know, at least, whether Fortuny has ever used as a decoration for his dressing gowns those pairs of birds, drinking in a vase, for example, which appear so frequently in St Mark's on Byzantine capitals? And do you know if in Venice there are any paintings (I would like some titles) in which any mantles or dresses appear that Fortuny may have (or could have) gained inspiration from?'[4] Maria having replied affirmatively, Proust could write with confidence that Albertine's dress, a gift from the narrator, 'swarmed with Arabic ornaments, like the Venetian palaces hidden like sultanas behind a screen of pierced stone, like the bindings in the Ambrosian library, like the columns from which the Oriental birds that symbolized alternatively life and death were repeated in the mirror of the fabric'.[5]

The world described by Proust, the world of high society, was dominated by rules, and everything – including dress – had a strictly delineated function that could not be altered. Sleek silk gowns like the Delphos, often worn with nothing underneath, were intended for use in the home. The least venturesome only wore them as dressing gowns or when *en deshabillé*;[6] in

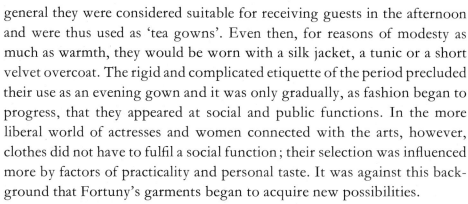

general they were considered suitable for receiving guests in the afternoon and were thus used as 'tea gowns'. Even then, for reasons of modesty as much as warmth, they would be worn with a silk jacket, a tunic or a short velvet overcoat. The rigid and complicated etiquette of the period precluded their use as an evening gown and it was only gradually, as fashion began to progress, that they appeared at social and public functions. In the more liberal world of actresses and women connected with the arts, however, clothes did not have to fulfil a social function; their selection was influenced more by factors of practicality and personal taste. It was against this background that Fortuny's garments began to acquire new possibilities.

Since Isadora Duncan had shown the need to reform dress before reforming dance, it was natural for Fortuny's clothes to be used by artists who were bringing about a rebirth of the dance and the theatre. In 1907 Ruth St Denis, who was beginning to enjoy great success with her Indian dances, wore Knossos scarves for a performance in Berlin.[7] This was not a random choice, for the Knossos scarf could be worn like a sari; it was of similar dimensions, and the symbolic decorations had an Oriental appearance. Isadora herself wore Fortuny dresses until her tragic death in 1927. She probably acquired her first when she visited Venice in 1910, but she had several and even commissioned a special miniature Delphos for her daughter Deirdre. La Duse, her great rival Emma Grammatica and later Martha Graham all employed Mariano's creations in their art in one form or another.

In 1909 Diaghilev's *Ballets Russes* made their first appearance in Paris, creating both scandal and legend with two opulent, colourful and exotic ballets, *Cléopâtre* and *Les Orientales*. The Oriental theme was continued in *Schéhérazade*, the sensational triumph of the 1910 season, and *Le Dieu Bleu* in 1912. The costumes by Bakst, Roerich and Goncharova were designed to be loose, and to allow maximum freedom of movement and expression. In this they followed the example of Isadora, whom Bakst and Diaghilev had met and admired during her Russian tour of 1906.[8] For the Greek ballets *Narcisse* (1911), *Daphnis et Chloë* (1912) and Nijinsky's scandalous *Après-Midi d'un Faune* (1912), Bakst re-interpreted the classical garment, Isadora's tunic and Fortuny's Delphos.

The *Ballets Russes* finally brought home the message preached so often by the Aesthetes. Its spectacular performances made a deep impression on the taste and sensibility of audiences, introducing a new aesthetic sense that rapidly extended beyond the stage. Cloaks, turbans and pantaloons became the new rage. Poiret's 'harem skirt' and 'lampshade tunic' were born. Interior

decorators filled their houses with cushions (a device already favoured by Fortuny), and used new materials richly decorated with Persian and other exotic designs. It was not long before fashion grasped the power and beauty of the new colours; intense, shocking and freely combined, they created new harmonies that supplanted the more restrained and limited colours in vogue at the time.

Mariano was likely to have seen *Schéhérazade* and *Carnaval* when they played as a double bill on 4 June 1910, for he had arrived in Paris only a few days earlier to obtain a patent on his new method of printing fabric. His cousin and childhood companion Coco de Madrazo was closely involved with the Russian ballet, and a year later, at the request of Diaghilev, prepared the libretto for *Le Dieu Bleu* with Jean Cocteau; Proust's friend Reynaldo Hahn composed the music. The costumes and scenery produced for the *Ballets Russes* were contemporary with Mariano's work and very much in the same spirit. As Proust wrote:

> 'Like the theatrical designs of Sert, Bakst, and Benoist who at that moment were recreating in the Russian ballet the most cherished moments of art – with the aid of works of art impregnated with their spirit and yet original – these Fortuny gowns, faithfully antique but markedly original, brought before the eye like a stage setting, with even greater suggestiveness than a setting, since the setting was left to the imagination, that Venice loaded with the gorgeous East from which they had been taken ...'[9]

It could even be said that Fortuny and the *Ballets Russes* had a mutual impact upon one another. The Delphos gowns and Venetian capes were already in existence by 1909, and Mariano's system of indirect lighting, invented several years before, had paved the way for the ballet's new stage designs. On the other hand, the innovations of the *Ballet Russes* reinforced Fortuny's fashions and greatly increased the demand for them. When Fortuny opened his Paris shop in 1920, the influence of the *Ballets Russes* was still very much alive and the names he chose for his different creations reflect this: the list of clothes in his promotional leaflet included such items as 'Schéhérazades', 'Persian jackets', 'Cut Velvet *Abbaias*' and 'Coptic or Saracen *Lustres*'. He also broadened the range of his pigments, introducing bright colours like orange, yellow and carmine.

Inevitably, Fortuny's fashions invite comparison with those of Paul Poiret. The two men resembled each other in a number of ways. Poiret too created a revolution. Like Mariano, he wanted to liberate women from the grip of the corset and reassert the natural shape of the body, and in about

Short jacket in lavender velvet stencilled in silver. (Countess Elsie Lee Gozzi, Venice/Gerard Amsellem)

Below: Lassitude, a 1912 drawing by Georges Barbier of a jacket and pleated dress by Paul Poiret, for Gazette de Bon Ton.

1907 he designed a series of dresses based on *Directoire* models. Interested in art and decoration, he organized a design workshop in 1911 where he printed materials with motifs by Dufy and other painters. He also created costumes for the stage, and his dresses possessed the slightly theatrical quality of Fortuny's which appealed to artistically inclined women like Ida Rubinstein, Mistinguett and, of course, Isadora Duncan. Poiret remained within the confines of fashion, however, and his obsession with extraneous details like buttons, bows and belts, prevented him from achieving the austere simplicity of Fortuny's clothing.

Poiret was a proud and eccentric man who refused to admit that he was affected by the ideas of others, but he clearly admired Fortuny's work and had Mariano's fabrics and dresses in his boutique. He provided each of his daughters with a Delphos robe,[10] and during the 1910s created his own version of the long, finely pleated gowns. A green silk chiffon tunic made by Fortuny was sold in his shop as early as 1908.[11] This is only significant because Poiret started to make use of such tunics at almost the same time as Mariano, and it is intriguing to note the similarity between Poiret's tunics in the George Barbier illustrations of 1908 and the Fortuny sold in 1908 which is now in the Union Française des Arts du Costume.

In 1907 Alfred Stieglitz took one of his first photographs in colour, a portrait of his sister, Selma Schubert, on a park bench in the autumn, wearing an old cardigan over a Delphos robe. This way of treating a

Opposite: Isadora Duncan in a drawing by Georges Barbier, 1917. The dress resembles the Delphos that she often wore. (Courtesy of Sotheby Parke Bernet, London)

Below: Four illustrations from Belle Armstrong Whitney's What to Wear: a Book for Women, *published in Battle Creek, Michigan in 1916. Americans were the first to wear Fortuny's garments outside the home. (Courtesy of Amanda Palmer, New York)*

Fortuny may seem much too casual, but it represents an important break with the sophistication that formed such an integral part of fashion and those who saw themselves as its arbiters. Ruth St Denis, Isadora Duncan and Selma Schubert were all Americans and Fortuny's influence soon spread to the United States. In May 1914 Mariano's dresses were exhibited at the Carroll Galleries in New York. Two years later, in a small Michigan town, a book was published entitled *What to Wear: a Book for Women*, written by Belle Armstrong Whitney; six of its nine illustrations showed dresses by Fortuny, while the remaining three were of dresses that fulfilled the same criteria. The text accompanying the illustrations expressed views similar to those held by the reformers of the late nineteenth century: 'Forty thousand members of the General Federation of Women's Clubs at a recent convention presented a set of resolutions denouncing modern fashions. They stigmatized them as "immodest, uncomfortable and unattractive".'[12] Belle Whitney considered Fortuny's dresses to fulfil all the conditions of her ideal dress, which in her view should be above fashion and change: efficiency, simplicity, personality, quality materials and a high standard of workmanship and artistry – 'the fabrics are exquisite, the colours such as painters love, the lines such as sculptors admire'.[13]

By 1916 many things had changed as regards dress, both within the realms of fashion and beyond. Fashion was developing along the lines laid down by Poiret and was therefore beginning to accept the criteria demanded by the reformers. Fortuny's dresses were in demand; as a result, a whole series of designers began to emerge who were familiar with Fortuny's work and had learned from him. Their dresses contained many Fortunyesque elements – sometimes too many – and museums and private collectors have been known to mistake their creations for those of Fortuny.

The first of these dressmakers was Maria Monaci Gallenga, who lived in Rome, where she was known as 'an artist of pre-Raphaelite tendencies'.[14] Like Fortuny, she progressed from art to dress and, dissatisfied with contemporary fashion, sought inspiration for her designs in the costumes of the past. There are too many ways in which her work coincides with that of Fortuny for it to be purely fortuitous. There are similarities in shape, cut and decorative motifs; she also used Venetian glass beads to give weight to her dresses, made velvet bags like Fortuny's, and even printed on velvet with medieval and Oriental designs in gold and silver. Her patterns, however, were generally bigger, less delicate than Mariano's, and the colours had a flatness that contrasted sharply with the texture and variety of his fabrics. Her vision of the past was obviously not original, but gained through her

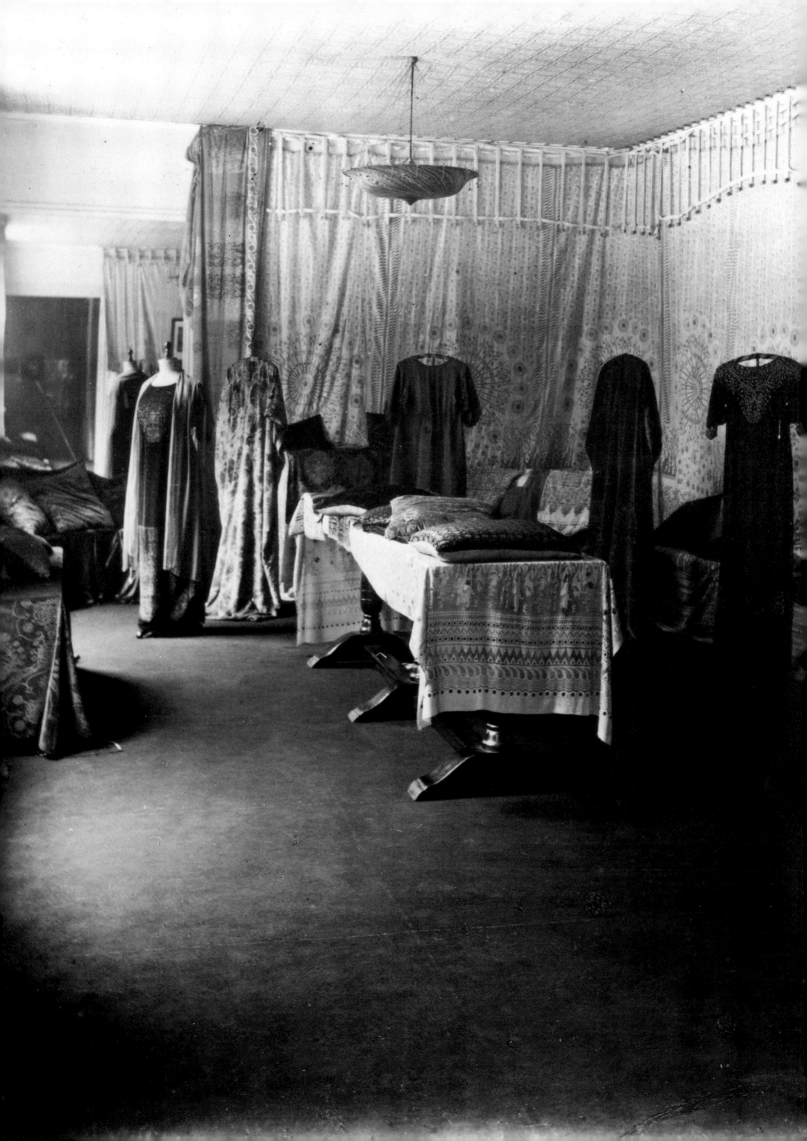

knowledge of Fortuny's work.

Another follower of Fortuny was Madame Babani. Around 1919 she opened a shop in Paris in the Boulevard Haussman which successfully sold his garments and materials as well as art fabrics from Liberty's of London, and Babani's own creations. Her dresses have occasionally been mistaken for Mariano's because she borrowed a number of ideas from him including his tunics, jibbahs, silk jackets and use of Arabic patterns. Babani worked with embroidered fabrics in addition to printed ones, a feature that differentiates her from Fortuny. She also employed bright colours that jumped out from the background, and both her materials and designs were less refined.

A third dressmaker who existed outside the world of *haute couture* was Madame Bertillon; her dresses, influenced by the *Ballets Russes*, Persia and the Orient, are clearly related to those of Fortuny.

None of these designers, however, succeeded in creating works of equal consequence to Fortuny's. Their dresses were of a similar *genre* and strove to be above the whims of fashion, but finally they lacked the enduring qualities that made Mariano's clothes unique.

The people of Europe continued to live normal lives, unaware of the cataclysm on the horizon. In Venice, many came to visit Fortuny's little shop on the ground floor of the Palazzo Orfei, and gazed in wonder at the dramatic array of mannequins dressed in his silks and velvets. Mariano and Henriette dedicated most of their time to work, but maintained contact with their close circle of friends. La Duse frequently dropped by for a chat, or to select a new costume. Fortuny remained friendly with the Hohenlohes and saw Régnier and D'Annunzio whenever they passed through Venice. The plan for a universal theatre had been revived at a meeting in Paris between Mariano and the Italian poet, but now the idea was to build it in the French capital instead of on Lake Albano. In 1912 they formed a society together with an architect by the name of Hess, and a member of the Rothschild family. Unfortunately D'Annunzio's erratic life-style made the project impossible and Fortuny was left to pursue it on his own.

Apart from a few trips abroad, mainly to Paris, Fortuny's life centred around the Palazzo Orfei, which is where he was when the First World War broke out. While the *Ballets Russes* toured Spain, America and other neutral countries, and the Dadaists began to reach Switzerland, Mariano decided to remain in Venice, determined that the war should not interfere with his way of life. After the Italians were put to rout at Caporetto, the city came increasingly under the threat of attack and many of its inhabitants began to move away. 'The bloody rumblings of July 1914 interrupted and overwhelmed

Detail of a silk taffeta wall hanging. Motif inspired by Cretan art; very similar to motifs in the Knossos veils. (Liselotte Höhs, Venice/E. Momeñe)

Opposite: The showroom of the Palazzo Orfei displaying Fortuny's dresses, textiles, cushions and lamps. Photograph by Mariano. (Museo Fortuny, Venice)

the *soirées*, the serenades, the ballets *à la Diaghilev*; everything was put to flight by the uncertainties of a twilight world.'[15]

When asked by an Italian politician whether he thought Venice ought to defend itself against an invasion, Fortuny replied that whatever happened he had no intention of leaving. This resolve was admirable but costly. As the war dragged on, the workshops ground to a halt, the family money was blocked abroad, and Mariano, who was running up large debts, had to mortgage his *palazzo*. The situation at the Palazzo Martinengo was equally distressing, and Doña Cecilia was forced to sell many of her precious objects. In a letter to her brother Ricardo, who was trying to help from Spain, she wrote: 'This war has been and is the downfall of everybody.'

Fortuny was an active member of the committee in charge of protecting Venetian art treasures and many priceless pieces were stored away in the Palazzo Orfei for safe-keeping during the war. In 1915 Mariano was made honorary Spanish consul, which technically placed the *palazzo* on neutral territory. Thereafter the ground floor, which already housed his dress shop, served the additional function of consular office: in one room there was a portrait of the Spanish King Alfonso XIII, and in another stood a royal court of mannequins.

Gabriele D'Annunzio was also in Venice; his flamboyant nature had led him to become an ardent supporter of Italy's intervention in the war, and he was now a fighter pilot based in Venice, near the front. Because of his popularity as a war hero it had become impossible for him to stay in hotels, so Fortuny contacted the Hohenlohe family, who had been forced to abandon Venice for Lugano, and persuaded them to let out the Casetta Rossa to D'Annunzio. It was the last time the two friends were to be together. Their lives had become very different and their paths did not cross again.[16]

The signing of the peace in 1918 signalled the return to normality. For the Palazzo Orfei, this meant starting production in the workshops once again, and the promise of better times ahead. In the same year Mariano decided at last to formalize his relationship with Henriette, and the two were quietly married after sixteen years of living together. The war, however, did more than interrupt the lives of its participants. After four terrible years of conflict the world had radically changed. The splendour of pre-war Venice was gone forever. The society described by Proust, the mannered world of the Guermantes, had been struck a mortal blow. New nations were emerging, new social credos, and with them a new style of life. Fortuny would have to respond accordingly.

Portrait of Henriette by Mariano, 1920. (Museo Fortuny, Venice/E. Momeñe)

VI

THE TWENTIES

Everyone went to Fortuny then. I think everyone I knew had a Fortuny dress.

LADY BONHAM-CARTER

Opposite: Fortuny at his easel, c. 1930. The easel, which he designed himself, was attached to a movable seat on rails. (Countess Elsie Lee Gozzi, Venice)

Below: Publicity pamphlet for Mariano's new textile company. The motif was taken from a sketchbook of textile designs by the 15th century Venetian painter Jacopo Bellini. (Countess Elsie Lee Gozzi, Venice)

During the 1920s Fortuny's name and work began to attract a much larger public. The cultured élite were no longer alone in wanting to wear his dresses and decorate their homes with his fabrics. The demand for his designs rose dramatically, and the small workshops in the Palazzo Orfei were incapable of satisfying it. Faced with the need to expand, Mariano decided to form a new company in 1919, called the Società Anonima Fortuny, and set up a factory devoted exclusively to the production of his own textiles. The delicate products that required the most work, such as the silk dresses and velvet coats, were still made in the Palazzo under the supervision of Henriette, but for the decorative trade Mariano began to experiment with less expensive materials.

There were good reasons for this decision. In the first place the market had changed radically since the pre-war years. Europe, already impoverished by the war, was still plagued by continual economic crises, and people wanted cheaper and more durable products. Design theorists were advocating a new approach to the applied arts. The Russian avant-garde had proposed austerity, functionalism and mass-production as solutions to their problems in 1917 after the Bolshevik Revolution, and these methods were now being advanced in the West by the De Stijl movement, the Bauhaus and, on a less intellectual level, by the exponents of Art Deco. While there was still room for luxury industries, the cost of both the velvet from Lyons and the silk from Japan had been seriously affected by inflation, and Mariano was forced to raise his prices sharply at a time when others were seeking to reduce theirs. More disturbingly, the economic difficulties had also made

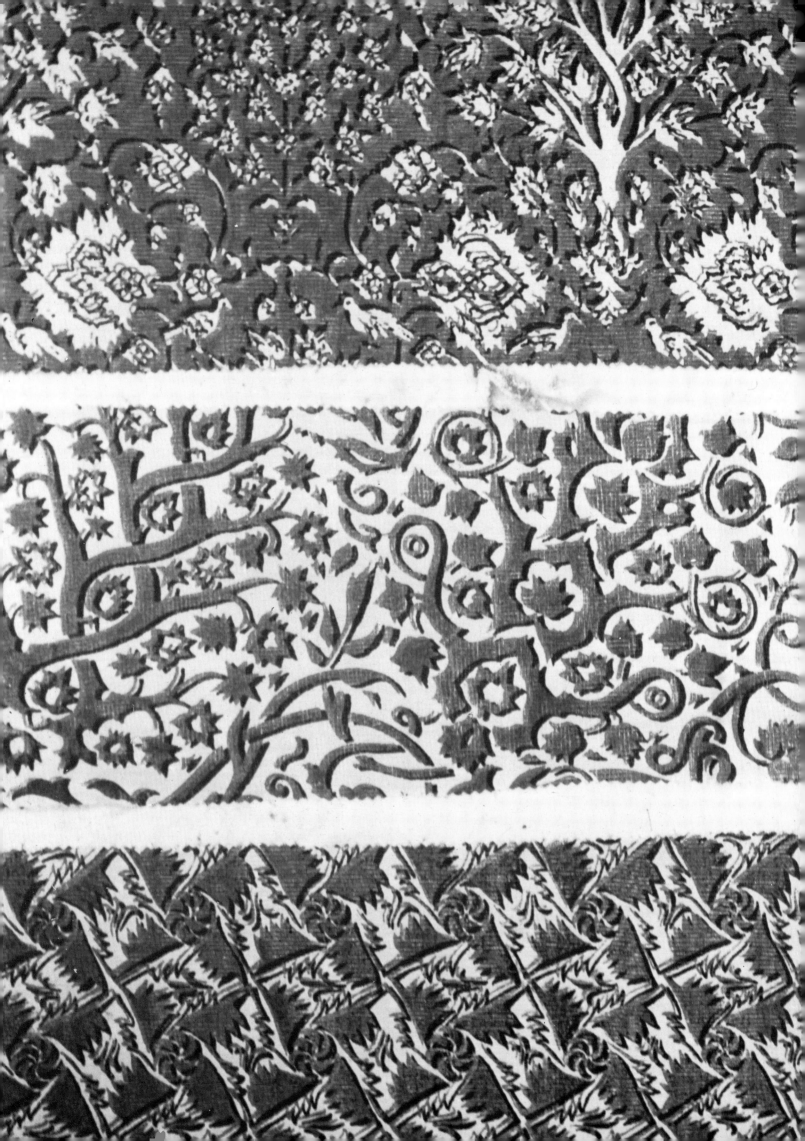

the raw materials more difficult to obtain, which implied an eventual reduction of output. Fortuny realized that failure to change with the times could prove fatal.

The factory was installed on the island of the Giudecca in an ancient convent that had been closed by Napoleon in the early 1800s. It was separated from the looming mass of the Stucky Wheat mill by a small canal, the Rio S. Biaggio. The convent and the large tracts of land on which it stood belonged to Giancarlo Stucky, a close friend of Mariano. Stucky was enormously wealthy and his mill, then the largest in the world, stretched from the Giudecca all the way to the Lagoon. With his friend's help, Fortuny converted the abandoned premises and installed the specialized machinery which he had himself invented for the purpose of carrying out his new ideas.

Work was begun in 1922. The first pieces of material were of long staple Egyptian cotton. Fortuny's entry into industrial production in no way involved lowering his standards. Although cotton called for a different technique, it still involved a high degree of manual labour, and the same artistic treatment of the material. Before being dyed, the cotton was washed to avoid further shrinkage. The printing technique was similar to that used for velvet and the goal was identical: a rich quality and depth of colour employing designs generally based on classical motifs. Mariano also experimented with linen, cotton velvets and raw silk, but none of these fabrics was sufficiently absorbent 'to give the beautiful effects we could obtain with long staple cotton'.[1] At the end of the twenties the type of cotton he

Opposite: Three samples of cotton with motifs inspired by Persian textiles. (Liselotte Höhs, Venice/E. Momeñe)

Workshop for screen and block printing on the top floor of the Palazzo Orfei. (Guillermo de Osma)

settled for was a one hundred per cent absorbent material manufactured in England by Tootal, Broadhurst, Lee of Manchester.

The Giudecca factory underlines Fortuny's enterprising spirit. He undertook responsibility for the whole process from designing the means of production, which he continually improved, to training a staff of one hundred people in a wide variety of skills; in fact he rarely employed an experienced worker or went outside the factory for technical assistance.

The new venture could only pay for itself by means of a much larger production output than was possible at the Palazzo Orfei. As a result, Fortuny found it necessary to extend his commercial network. In 1920 he opened his own shop in Paris at 67 rue Pierre Charron, almost on the corner of the Champs Elysées, beside Paul Poiret's boutique, *Rosine*. The façade of the shop appeared modern and austere, but inside it was a continuation of the *palazzo*: 'Whichever way one turns, one discovers nothing but over-hanging lengths of cloth, in very warm and subtle shades, enriched with magical ornamentation. It is really bewitching. One feels that some tale from the Thousand and One Nights is going to unfold against this decorative background, or perhaps some scene from Renaissance Venice.'[2] Aside from his dresses, velvets and printed cottons, Fortuny had produced a whole series of household furnishings made out of his own materials:

cushions, screens, painted silk lampshades and a variety of wall hangings. There were even metal desk lamps using reflecting light, which were so simply designed that they seem perfectly modern today.

In Italy Fortuny had another retail outlet, in Milan, and representatives in Turin, Genoa, Rome and Naples. His work was also sold in Madrid, Zurich, London and New York. Mrs Ralph Sanger and Mrs James Freeman Curtis introduced his designs into America in 1923 when they opened The Brick Shop above Lexington Avenue in Manhattan. There, among the international luxury goods, in 'a little brocade-hung room piled with samples of that deceptive printed cotton that you can't believe until you see it', shoppers could discover the same exotic environment that existed in Paris.[3] In the same year Ethel Barrymore wore a Fortuny dress for the title role in *Romeo and Juliet* staged by the Long Acre Theatre in New York, and soon other Hollywood stars of the 1920s and 1930s like Lillian Gish and Dolores del Rio began to appear in his gowns both on and off the screen.

Fortuny's cotton fabrics became very popular and were widely used for decorative purposes because of their ability to blend harmoniously with almost anything. Mariano was frequently asked to advise well-known socialites like Consuelo Vanderbilt and Dina Galli on the decoration of their houses and as a result began studying the problems of interior design.

In about 1920 he decorated the gaming rooms of the Hotel Excelsior on the Lido of Venice. He did not paper the walls, but hung materials like enormous curtains from rails placed just below ceiling level. Their folds gave a feeling of movement and warmth to the rooms, as well as producing a play of light that heightened their colour.

The cotton fabrics also proved a great success in the decoration of museums and large exhibition halls, forming the background for paintings and other *objets d'art*. They were printed with a great number of different designs, based on motifs from the same periods as the pictures and furniture being exhibited, and dyed in muted shades that provided an ideal foil for the artwork. Fortuny himself had for many years hung his own paintings this way in the Palazzo Orfei.

In the 1924 Biennale exhibition in Venice, Fortuny repeated the technique he had used in the Hotel Excelsior when designing the Spanish pavilion. Later in the year his materials were used to decorate the rooms in the Monza exhibition commemorating the painter Mose Bianchi. In 1926 he once more provided the decor for the Spanish pavilion in Venice, and in the following year designed part of the Esposizione Morelli and the Titian rooms for the Museum of Naples. During the same period his fabrics

*Above: Man Ray photograph of the
dancer Catherine Hawley, a pupil of
Isadora Duncan, wearing a velvet gown
with pleated silk insets by Fortuny.
(Sea Cliff Photograph Co.)*

*Opposite: Lillian Gish in a Delphos
(Neill Dorr)*

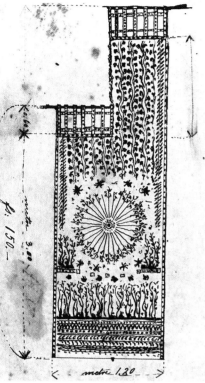

Above: One of the few surviving drawings by Fortuny: a wall hanging with instructions for its display. (Countess Elsie Lee Gozzi, Venice)

decorated the Spanish pavilion at the Milan Fair, the rooms in the Rome Biennale, and even the interior of a church, the Chiesa del Redentore in Venice.

François Boucher, associate curator of the Carnavalet Museum in Paris, asked Mariano to help him redesign the museum, which was being expanded and given a whole new image. Boucher was later given credit for turning it into a museum of international importance. He had been looking for a high-quality fabric that was less expensive than velvet, and provided Fortuny with detailed information about the rooms and the colours that he wanted. In response, the artist created a successful pattern that managed to incorporate the museum's name.

The new materials were also employed in theatres, both for stage curtains and for scenery. In 1926 when Emma Grammatica produced George Bernard Shaw's *St Joan*, she decided to use Fortuny's printed cottons as almost the only decorative device in the production: as the backcloth, as part of the scenery and also to make some of the dresses worn by the heroine, played by Emma herself. The theatre had helped to crystallize Mariano's conception of dress, and he now returned the favour by offering it a way of staging productions at a much lower cost. Period costumes could now be made of much cheaper materials, but still achieve a similar effect.

It is strange that the twenties should have been such a fruitful period for Fortuny; they were also the years of Art Deco, short skirts, post-Cubism, Dada, Jazz, Surrealism and Joyce – a far cry from his fascination with

Right: Emma Grammatica's 1926 production of George Bernard Shaw's St Joan, *which used Fortuny's materials as almost the only decorative device. (Countess Elsie Lee Gozzi, Venice)*

Fashion magazines began to acknowledge
Fortuny during the 1920s.
Above: English society lady in a
Delphos from the June 1920 issue of
American Vogue. (*Charlotte
Fairchild photograph of Miss Horatia
Seymour/Courtesy* VOGUE, *copyright
© 1923, 1951 by The Condé Nast
Publications Inc.*)
Left: Illustration from a 1927 issue of
British Vogue *which carried the
caption,* 'All the poetry of line of the
Greek robe has been preserved in this
finely pleated tea-gown of very soft grey-
blue satin which slips on over the head
and draws up in the shoulders.'
(*Photograph by Maurice Beck and
Macgregor,* © *The Condé Publications
Ltd.*)

Classical themes. His own modern designs were curvilinear and exotic and somewhat reminiscent of Art Nouveau, but he made use of geometrical patterns, some inspired by Arab art and others of small, alternating dark and light squares, which may have been inspired by architectural motifs.

At the Exposition des Arts Décoratifs in Paris in 1925, which proclaimed the triumph of Art Deco, Fortuny exhibited mainly fabrics (although in the catalogue he was classed as a painter), and was probably unique in showing work under two different flags, since one of the rooms in the Italian pavilion was decorated with his materials. Other outstanding textile works in the Spanish pavilion were the fabrics of the Catalan, Tomás Aymat, and the batiks of Perez Dolç, which were exhibited alongside various pieces of velvet by Fortuny, including a wallhanging printed with the Spanish coat-of-arms. Maria Gallenga exhibited some of her materials, and certain avant-garde designers took part as well, such as the Futurist Depero, Guido Ravasi and Carlo Piatti, who had received acclaim at the Decorative Arts Biennale in Monza.

Although Mariano's dresses had anticipated many features of the twenties' fashions, he was not invited to show his work in the fashion pavilion, which had been organized by and for *modistes*. Fashion had been forced to develop in the same direction as Fortuny, but for different reasons. During the war women had substituted for men, and to some extent adopted their way of dressing, and they were not prepared to abandon their new status with the advent of peace. Yet there was more to it than that. The period had witnessed a complete change in social customs. 'To come and go as she wished, to sit in her open sports car, play tennis, and then perform the fox-trot at some *thé dansant*, a woman had to dispense with all unnecessary clutter. A simple combination garment had taken the place of the corset. Dresses were no longer fitted; they left the body free and no longer clung tightly to the neck and arms.'[4] The different styles of dress were suddenly reduced to two: day wear and evening wear. Art, too, had played an important part in these developments; the sensational discovery of the tomb of Tutankhamun, the colonial exhibitions, African art and Cubism had all made a contribution.

Fortuny dresses enjoyed an enormous success during the 1920s. Fashion magazines at last began to acknowledge their existence, and illustrations appeared in their pages, albeit infrequently. People were familiar with Mariano's dresses, particularly the Delphos gowns, and if they were not wearing them, they were certainly discussing them. 'Everybody went to Fortuny then. I think everyone I knew had a Fortuny dress',[5] recalls Lady

Illustration for an article entitled 'The Beauty of Fortuny is Brought to America', which appeared in the May 1923 issue of Vogue. *(Wynn Richards photograph courtesy* VOGUE, *copyright © 1923, 1951 by Condé Nast Publications Inc.)*

Opposite: Mrs Condé Nast, c. 1919, in a Delphos and long mantle. She was the wife of the publisher who founded Vogue *magazine. (Copyright © 1979 Aurum Press Ltd.)*

From a *1927* issue of British Vogue:
Delphos and matching velvet mantle,
lyrically described as having 'a darker
tone of grey-blue with a suggestion of
peacock as it catches the light'.
(Photograph by Maurice Beck and
Macgregor. © *The Condé Nast*
Publications Ltd.)

Opposite: Wynn Richards photograph
of Nazimova in a Delphos and velvet
coat. (Courtesy VOGUE, *copyright* ©
1923, 1951 by the Condé Nast
Publications Inc.)

Mariano's library in the Palazzo Orfei where he kept a vast archive of photographs in separate fabric-covered volumes, and his manual press. Covering the table are etchings by his father and himself. (Countess Elsie Lee Gozzi, Venice)

Bonham-Carter, Miss Charlotte Ogilvy at the time. In 1920 she travelled with her mother to Venice, and went shopping with her at the Palazzo Orfei. Mrs Ogilvy bought a black velvet cloak, while her daughter bought a Delphos that she continued to wear for the next ten years and which she has now, at the age of eighty, brought out to use once more.

After the war there was a new surge of Eastern influence on the world of fashion, which according to *Vogue* was due to the homecoming soldiers bringing with them ethnic dresses and materials. Fortuny's Eastern-inspired cloaks and capes combined perfectly with the caftans, burnouses and jibbahs being worn by Parisian ladies. Everyone was fascinated by the pleats of the Delphos. By 1910 Poiret had already created long pleated dresses that recalled Fortuny's work, but now Callot and Lanvin were using the same kind of small pleats in some of their models. In 1923 *Vogue*, commenting on a Lanvin dress, said that 'pleating is so important that it has come into the summer evening mode'. Fortuny's dresses still seemed somehow too simple in comparison with contemporary evening wear and were rarely worn at night. However, women loved to be painted and photographed wearing Fortunys (Muriel Gore wore a Fortuny dress for her portrait by Sir Oswald Binley in 1919) and some were married in his white gowns. In this way Mariano's work attracted an ever greater number of admirers.

Opposite: Mrs Muriel Gore in a Delphos and velvet cloak, painted in 1919 by the fashionable English portrait painter Sir Oswald Binley. (Courtesy of Sotheby Parke Bernet, London)

Fortuny with Spanish artist Benlliure during his trip to Spain in 1929 to discuss the installation of his cyclorama at the Teatro Real of Madrid. (Countess Elsie Lee Gozzi, Venice)

Opposite: 2 designs for cotton. Lucrezia (top), a 17th century Italian style design named after the Rembrandt painting; Persepolis (bottom), a Persian inspired design.

In Madrid, Mariá de Cardona, a writer and intellectual, did much to popularize Fortuny dresses and materials. She had known Mariano in Venice when he was still a young man; her father had been part of the entourage of Don Carlos, the Carlist pretender to the Spanish throne, and she herself had been lady-in-waiting to his wife Doña Berta de Rohan. Thanks to María de Cardona a number of palaces in Madrid were decorated with Fortuny's textiles.[6] Around 1930 some of the rooms in the Museo Naval were decorated with his cottons, and later Madrid University commissioned various pieces of velvet from him.

Despite this expansion of activities which occurred at a particularly difficult time, the atmosphere in the Orfei remained unchanged. The spirit of work, peace and cloistered unreality still reigned supreme: 'thus, in the year of 1922, surrounded on all sides by financial hardship, misery and shortages, this Venetian Spaniard of Catalan Venetian found himself living in the midst of Arabian Nights luxury as a result of the needs of his work.'[7] The author, Ugo Ojetti, adds a vivid description of the artist at this time:

'He has not changed during the thirty years that I have known him, except for the silver in his bristly and neatly-barbered black beard. And the strangest thing is that if I try and remember what he looks like, I can only visualize him full on, face to face with the person he is speaking to, his hands in his pockets, his head held high and a half-smile on his lips, somewhere between the cordial and the unconventional. And this is how he is inside: clear-headed and lion-hearted, accustomed to face up to difficulties quietly and resolutely, treating them as a problem of optics and mechanics like a German bombardment.'[8]

During the years in which Fortuny was paying special attention to research and manufacture in the field of textiles, he continued to develop his interest in photography, incorporating it into his work by taking pictures of natural patterns which he subsequently enlarged and used for tracing designs. Neither did he abandon painting. In 1919 he took part in the exhibition of Spanish contemporary art in Paris organized by Mariano Benlliure with the help of Fortuny's cousin, Mariano de Madrazo, and between 1922 and 1940 he participated in most of the Venice Biennales. It is interesting to note that in 1922, when Mariano was himself responsible for organizing the Spanish pavilion, he presented his father's etchings side by side with his own work and that of other contemporary artists.

During the 1920s Fortuny's contribution to the theatre gained widespread recognition. He had spent a great deal of time improving his dome,

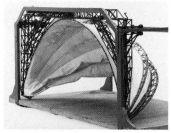

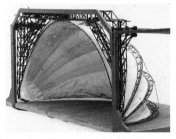

Scale model (100 × 80 cm) of the mobile cyclorama which the Italian company Leonardo da Vinci installed in the Milan opera house, La Scala, in 1922. (Countess Elsie Lee Gozzi, Venice)

and it was now used in many theatres, notably in France, Germany and Russia, Italy, however, was the first to grasp its full potential, and his efforts were crowned by the installation of a large dome in the country's most famous opera house, La Scala of Milan. The theatre's technical committee wanted it to be constructed to their own specifications, and hired a Milanese firm, the Società Leonardo da Vinci, to build it. Fortuny was assisted by a young engineer called Silvio Bassi and a whole team of technicians employed to solve the enormous practical problems involved. The dome was essentially the same model as had been installed in the Paris theatre in the Avenue Bosquet in 1906, but whereas the first one measured 12 metres in diameter, the new one had to be 22 metres. It was composed of white, sized cotton of the kind used for Zeppelins, stretched over a metal framework that contained the various functional and support mechanisms. The dome was electrically controlled and could fold and unfold like a giant accordion in the space of 90 seconds. It also moved along rails, covering 16 metres in 75 seconds; both manoeuvres were completely silent. To keep the structure taut Fortuny had invented a suction fan which drew out the air through a tube 1.5 metres in diameter by means of an electrical motor.

The dome was inaugurated on 7 January 1922 with a production of Fortuny's favourite Wagnerian opera, *Parsifal*. The lights reflected against the white cupola and enveloped the whole stage, creating an atmosphere which must surely have fulfilled the composer's dream of uniting painting, music and drama. For some time, however, Mariano's thoughts had been turning back to his old idea of a universal theatre that would revitalize dramatic art. He had already drawn up several plans for D'Annunzio at the beginning of the century, and now started working on a large *maquette* of the project.[9]

This scale model reproduced Fortuny's vision in detail. It revealed an enormous amphitheatre, capable of being adapted to every kind of spectacle, which bore traces of Greek and Roman influence and recalled elements of Palladio's Olympic Theatre in Vicenza. The back of the auditorium was bounded by a great open *loggia* adorned with statues. An awning, like the *velarium* of ancient Roman theatres, retained sound and protected the spectators from bad weather, but was also designed to control the natural light, acting as an additional stage effect. The theatre included the Fortuny dome and indirect lighting system, 'thereby succeeding in transferring, in the field of lighting, that concept of an association between the stage (action) and the public, which in the Greek theatre was constituted by the orchestra (chorus)'.[10] The dome enclosed the whole stage, but an opening at the centre

let in natural light from overhead that could be made to work with the artificial light in the theatre, to produce harmonies and contrasts both on the stage and in the auditorium. It was to be, in Fortuny's words, 'a theatre in the sky, where people feel really out of this world'.[11]

In 1929 Mariano travelled to Montjuich, outside Barcelona, where he studied the possibility of actually building his great theatre, but the political situation in Spain proved too uncertain, and he was once again prevented from bringing to life his most ambitious project. The Spanish had become interested in his lighting system as well and on the same journey he visited the architect Antonio Flores of the Teatro Real in Madrid with a view to installing it there. However, this venture also failed to materialize, there being too many problems involved in transforming the old theatre, and Fortuny had to return to Venice empty-handed.

In Italy an intriguing new project awaited Fortuny. A travelling theatre company called the Carro di Tespi (The Thespian Cart) had been founded with the support of the Fascist Ministry of Culture, who saw it as a

Scale models for Mariano's 'ideal' theatre. The enormous amphitheatre was designed to include his cyclorama and indirect lighting system. (Museo Fortuny, Venice/E. Momeñe)

Theatre designed by Fortuny for a travelling company called the Carro di Tespi (The Thespian Cart), which was inaugurated in Rome in 1929 with a production of Alfieri's Oreste *and a comedy by Forzano. (Museo Fortuny, Venice)*

way of bringing culture to the far-flung corners of the nation and accelerating the process whereby 'a theatre for the *bourgeoisie* would be supplanted by a theatre for the masses'.[12] Its director, Giovacchino Forano, wanted to use Mariano's dome for a stage on wheels. The Fortuny dome and lighting system eliminated the need for painted scenery and thus resolved the major problem of limited storage space. Mariano adapted his system to the particular needs of the company by making the dome serve both as a backdrop and a means of supporting the awnings. In July 1929 the Carro di Tespi put on its first performance in Rome. It was an occasion of great national pride and Mussolini himself was in the audience. Mariano and Henriette sat directly behind him chatting with one another in French. As the curtain rose, the dictator turned around in his seat to glare at these foreigners who had somehow intruded upon the scene; apparently nobody had thought to introduce him to the man who invented the theatre!

It is a testament to Mariano's genius that after thirty years, and the enormous advances in stage-lighting techniques which had taken place in the interim, his dome and its indirect lighting system were still going strong. As Alberto Spaini wrote in 1919: 'One could easily bet that Fortuny, whose mind, in order of precedence, stands somewhere between Goethe and Edison, has never suffered the slightest displeasure from his skies, his lights, his colours.'[13]

Opposite: Fortuny before the theatre of the Carro di Tespi with Giovannino Forzano, the company's director. Rome 1929. (Museo Fortuny, Venice)

VII

THE FINAL YEARS

What an enviable inner life Mariano Fortuny has lived, and is still living each day, amidst the paradise of his dreams come true.

MIGUEL ZAMACOIS

Mariano in a photograph dedicated by him to Elsie McNeill, later Countess Gozzi, in 1930. (Countess Elsie Lee Gozzi, Venice)

The 1930s were trying years for Mariano. He was by now receiving a good income from the sale of his dresses and fabrics, but was no longer wealthy, having spent a large portion of the family fortune in realizing his many projects. Then came the Wall Street Crash of 1929. The Great Depression that followed spread hardship and ruin across Europe and America, and for Mariano a difficult situation was intensified by the actions of a dishonest administrator. Mariano fought to keep going, and during the ensuing struggle discovered an invaluable ally in the attractive young American, Elsie McNeill.

McNeill was an interior decorator with a flair for business. She was just starting her very successful career when she became aware of Fortuny through Mrs Curtis and her Manhattan Brick Shop. In 1927 she visited the newly remodelled Carnavalet Museum in Paris, and was entranced by the quality and colours of the Fortuny materials. From there she went on to Venice, and met Mariano, persuading him to give her the exclusive rights to sell his goods in the United States. It was a fateful agreement, and the beginning of a long and fruitful relationship.

Upon her return to New York, McNeill chose the premises for a new shop at 509 Madison Avenue, in a building nearing completion. She then approached Arthur H. Lee and Sons Inc., a wholesale textile company with a large outlet in New York and further offices and representatives throughout the United States. It was agreed that they would handle the importation, storage and distribution of the cotton material, and that the profit from all

sales made through their offices would be divided with Elsie McNeill Inc. on an equal basis. Any other sales were strictly the shop's. The arrangements proved very satisfactory. On her second trip to Italy, McNeill was accompanied by the firm's president, Humphrey Lee, who helped her select appropriate materials for the American market. As it happened, the two fell in love and were eventually married. Elsie Lee continued as an interior designer, frequently using Fortuny fabrics in her work, and promoting them across the country through her membership in the American Institute of Decorators. The shop did very well, for it was the first time an art fabric was offered to decorators at reasonable prices. Even the dresses were comparatively inexpensive: the price of a Delphos was 125 dollars, which was much less expensive than a *couture* gown of the period.

Henriette Fortuny in a photograph dedicated by her to Elsie McNeill, later Countess Gozzi, in 1930. (Countess Elsie Lee Gozzi, Venice)

Elsie now travelled regularly to Venice to meet Mariano and discuss the problems of decoration and American sales. She suggested the idea of making a long-sleeved version of the Delphos for evening occasions and encouraged him to put an extra width of material in the narrow gowns so that more women could wear them. To avoid paying a luxury import tax, the dresses arrived in New York 'unassembled', and were therefore treated as lengths of material by the customs authorities. The various elements were then sewn together by a French dressmaker Elsie found for the purpose: the pieces of pleated silk, the Venetian glass beads, and the cords for adjusting the fit. The gowns were rolled up in a ball, and like Fortuny she sold them in small hat boxes with a leaflet explaining how best to look after them: 'Your gown each time after wearing should be twisted somewhat as you now find it. In order to preserve the life of the gown, we would suggest that it be sent to us for cleaning.' The dresses were made up in a special deartment in the Madison Avenue premises; another department undertook repairs and alterations.

If the situation looked promising in America, the reverse was true in Italy. With the advent of the Depression, the Stucky enterprises, including the great wheat mill, began to suffer heavy losses. Large loans had to be obtained by Stucky from a Milan bank; when these could not be repaid bankruptcy was declared, and a Receiver appointed to liquidate the assets of the various concerns within a period of three years. Although the details of any agreement between Giancarlo Stucky and Fortuny are not known, the Giudecca factory was clearly involved. Apart from owning the land, Stucky apparently had a number of shares in S.A. Fortuny as well, and Mariano, writing to Humphrey Lee in 1933, declared that the entire Giudecca property including the machinery and raw materials had been placed in receivership.

Opposite: Elsie McNeill at the age of 20 in a Delphos and grenadine coat. (Countess Elsie Lee Gozzi, Venice)

This naturally affected the whole operation, and in the same letter he added: 'The situation is becoming very serious for me, and I must make great reductions in my Paris shop, which breaks my heart, but I hope that the world will not stop turning, and that things will pick up again.' [1]

Matters did not improve, however, and by the following year Fortuny was in further trouble. Although the *palazzo* workshops were a separate enterprise, and work in silk and velvet continued to be produced there as before, Mariano wrote: 'Things are extremely bad and we are living from day to day, very worried about the future of the Orfei where I am once more having to lay off members of the workforce.' [2]

The Lees had offered to retrieve the Giudecca factory from its creditors and Fortuny was delighted, but he warned them that it was not going to be easy to get the business back on its feet again. 'I think that for a long time it would be wise to shut the factory, leaving only three technicians needed to look after the machinery there, who could also be employed to safeguard and gradually sell off the cottons – I am under no illusion concerning the factory's recovery which will certainly be a very, very slow and laborious process.' [3]

What Fortuny failed to realize at the time was the fact that his trusted administrator was stealing large sums of money from the company funds, so turning a difficult situation into a desperate one. When this treachery was finally uncovered, the poor man burned the meticulous records of his theft, and committed suicide.

In the end the bank rejected the Lees' offer to buy S.A. Fortuny, either because the bankruptcy proceedings had gone too far or because it hoped to take control of the company for its own purposes. The Receiver for the bankrupt Stucky estate took a keen interest in Elsie Lee, however, and clearly hoped to gain her support for the take-over. He invited her to dinner, sent flowers, and even telephoned her on shipboard (an exceptional gesture in those days), all of which was reported to Fortuny. He then embarked on a lengthy correspondence with her, attempting to secure detailed information about the American operation. When the time came for the Giudecca factory to be auctioned, it emerged that Fortuny, as principal shareholder, had the right to make the first bid for its recovery. The bank itself would make a sealed counter-bid. Countess Gozzi, then Elsie Lee, recalls how the factory was saved: 'The Receiver cabled me the bank's bid. Why he cabled it, I'll never know. Mr Fortuny was about to leave for the meeting when my message arrived giving the figure.' [4] Mercifully, the bank's offer was low, and Fortuny was able to exceed it. The Giudecca factory was back in his hands. It was still a difficult time, but the worst was over, and with the pleated dresses and velvets selling well in spite of the Depression, Mariano returned to work with renewed determination.

The uncertain future of Fortuny's textile production did not prevent him from engaging in other activities during the early 1930s. In 1931, for example, he invented a type of carbonized paper for making photographic prints which Zeiss Ikon, the camera company, were very interested in manufacturing.[5] In the same year he prepared the sets for Wagner's *Die Meistersinger*, portraying with equal skill the narrow medieval streets in the second act, and the open spaces of the great esplanade where the final singing contest takes place. The opera opened in Rome at the same theatre where thirty years earlier Mariano had designed the costumes and scenery for D'Annunzio's *Francesca da Rimini*. Formerly the Teatro Costanzi, it had been renamed The Royal Opera House in 1928 after extensive remodelling, and now boasted a very up-to-date lighting system designed by Ettore Salani, following Fortuny's lead.

During this period, owing to the financial straits in which he found himself, Fortuny decided to market his tempera colours. In 1933, the French painter René Piot wrote an article on the quality of these paints:

'This year my friend Mariano Fortuny sent me his tempera colours, and I hesitated before embarking on some fruitless trial. After using them, however, I found them so admirable that I now use only this kind of tempera . . . The clays are washed in Verona, but Mariano Fortuny is in the process of installing, in his wonderful Palazzo Orfei in Venice, a whole series of large basins for washing the colours, copied from the prototype that he found in the back of a shop and bought in 1895 following the death of an old apothecary in Mantua, who was perhaps a descendant of the one that sold Romeo his poison.'[6]

For forty years Mariano had continued to improve his technique of making pigments and dyes, and like the old Venetian masters he admired, never confided his methods to anyone. As Degas once remarked, 'You must remember, Monsieur, that during the good old days the artists had their secrets, and also a dagger to defend them.'[7] Now, however, the circumstances and age in which he lived forced Fortuny to make his secrets public property. He had perfected two types of tempera: a light one similar to that used by Dürer and Carpaccio, particularly the latter, and a very strong one which could be applied thickly without cracking. The range of colours he achieved was enormous. There were, for example, four kinds of white:

silvery white, *blanc de Chine*, zinc white and titanium white. Over the years Mariano continually added new colours to his palette, which included a number of rare shades no longer in common use.

Fortuny's innovations in the realm of painting were not restricted to his pigments. He also prepared his canvas in a special way, invented a type of easel with a seat attached to it which moved along small rails so that the painter could inspect his work easily from different distances, and built his own sort of scaffolding for painting or restoring ceilings. Mariano seemed to regard self-sufficiency as almost a moral principle for an artist.

In order to show the quality of his tempera colours, Fortuny held two large exhibitions; one in 1934 at the Galerie Hector Brame in Paris, and the other in November 1935 at the Galleria Dedalo in Milan. They were the only one-man shows of his life. In Paris Mariano displayed just thirty-two pictures – in oil, tempera and watercolour – but the Milan exhibition represented a true anthology of his work. There were ninety-two exhibits in all, which included engravings, drawings, and paintings as well as velvets and printed cotton fabrics. On show were his earliest portraits of María Luisa and Princess Hohenlohe side by side with his latest series of Henriette. There were views of Morocco, Venetian landscapes, scenes from Shakespeare and Wagner, nudes, still-lives, several designs for stained glass windows, and copies of Tintorettos and Tiepolos. Introducing the catalogue, his friend Miguel Zamacois wrote: 'How, after undertaking a tour of this attractive and varied exhibition, can one not feel the respect due to this man who, with a complete and extremely rare sense of impartiality, is at the same time both artist and artisan in the noblest meaning of the words . . . What

Opposite: Fortuny's retrospective exhibition at the Galleria Dedalo in Milan, 1935. The walls of the gallery were decorated for the occasion with material in a 17th century Italian style design called Olympia. *(Countess Elsie Lee Gozzi, Venice)*

Left: Exhibition of Fortuny's textiles at the Galleria Dedalo, Milan in 1935. (Countess Elsie Lee Gozzi, Venice)

Far left: Curtain made from Fortuny fabrics in a Viennese theatre. (Countess Elsie Lee Gozzi, Venice)

Cecilia Fortuny photographed by Mariano at the Palazzo Martinengo shortly before her death in 1932. (Countess Elsie Lee Gozzi, Venice)

Portrait of Cecilia Fortuny at the age of 84 by her son Mariano, 1928. It was exhibited in the Venice Biennale of 1950. (Museo Fortuny, Venice/E. Momeñe)

an enviable inner life Mariano Fortuny has lived, and is still living each day, amidst the paradise of his dream come true.'[8]

The exhibition generated a great deal of interest and, in happier times, could have offered a partial solution to Mariano's financial problems, but as he himself wrote: 'It has been a very big success, but with very few sales unfortunately. There is no business; the people are too worried.'[9] The crisis was a general one, affecting not only Fortuny. Italy, together with the rest of Europe, was in a critical condition and the radical ideologies that arose as a result would soon precipitate the Continent into the Second World War.

Mariano's personal worries were never revealed in the numerous articles which were written about him at the time. The press spoke glowingly of his achievements, and presented him in the same enviable light that he appeared to Zamacois. Yet there was a constant note of sadness to this period of Fortuny's life. Within the space of a few years he lost three of the people closest to him. His mother died in August 1932. In Mariano's last portrait of her in 1928, when she was already eighty-four years old, Doña Cecilia appears to retain all the qualities which Boldini's picture had captured many years before. Elegant, dignified, determined, she was perhaps the single greatest influence in Fortuny's life. Mariano's beautiful book on his father's work, published a year after her death, was an appropriate homage to her memory.

María Luisa, alone now in the vast halls of the Palazzo Martinengo, survived her mother by only a few years. Her death in 1936 was, in addition, preceded by that of Mariano's cousin and childhood friend, Coco de Madrazo. Of those who had shared Mariano's life, only Henriette remained.

In 1933 Mariano began work on the sets for Manuel de Falla's *La Vita Breve* which opened at La Scala on 15 January 1934. His designs were executed by Pietro Stroppa who had previously worked for Eleonora Duse, Emma Grammatica, and D'Annunzio. The work was set in Granada, and in the second scene, Fortuny paid a sentimental tribute to his birthplace with a panoramic view of the city, dominated by the Alhambra. At La Scala he was of course working with his own diffuse lighting system which was ideal for recreating the clear, hot and boundless light of Andalusia. The following year, Fortuny was called upon at the last moment to prepare the costumes and lighting for a production of *Othello* which was set to open shortly in Venice. The play, directed by Pietro Sharoff and starring Marta Palmer, was not to be staged in a conventional theatre, but in the grandiose courtyard of the Doges Palace, a very difficult place in which to achieve effective stage-lighting. There was little time, but Mariano resolved the problem by creating a series of luminous areas which produced an interplay of light and shadow across the courtyard. The costumes he described as follows: 'For the first act an Eastern djellaba, a coffee-coloured and green Venetian tunic; for the act that takes place in Cyprus something in the style of Carpaccio . . . a loose red gown with stockings of the same colour. But later on a more simple effect, with a white and grey tunic.'[10]

Unfortunately, Mariano's problems off-stage were less tractable. In 1936 the Italian government, in a fit of patriotic zeal, decided to promote industrial self-sufficiency by prohibiting the importation of many raw

Portrait of Henriette in a rose-coloured Delphos and Knossos scarf. Tempera on panel. It is dedicated 'to my wife' and dated 1935. (Museo Fortuny, Venice/E. Momeñe)

materials from abroad, amongst which were silk and velvet. Fortuny had always worked with Japanese silk because of its high quality and he knew its possibilities and limitations. A change of fabric meant altering his whole system of dyeing, pleating and manufacture. In addition he felt that Italian silk was unreliable: 'One moment it is very good and the next it is anything but! So I must have Japanese silk.'[11] Before the embargo was imposed he had ordered fifty lengths of silk. These were now being held by the Italian

The sets for Manuel de Falla's La Vita Breve *(The Short Life) designed by Fortuny and executed by Pietro Stroppa. The opera was staged at La Scala, Milan in 1934.*

customs authorities who refused to allow them into the country. Having tried unsuccessfully to show that it was impossible to obtain silk of the same quality in Italy, Fortuny turned once more to Elsie Lee for help. He thought that if the silk were quickly shipped to America he might have a better chance of reimporting it from there. Elsie would have to attach a document, however, stating that this was the only quality of silk which could be used to make the Delphos robes she had commissioned from Italy. 'Without that [the silk] I do not know what to do; the Delphos is virtually my only source of income.'[12]

Opposite: Elsie McNeill photographed by Fortuny in a Delphos with long sleeves, and a silk gauze wrap, c. 1927. (Countess Elsie Lee Gozzi, Venice)

Model photographed by Fortuny in the 1930s: Silk coat with very wide sleeves, the motifs inspired by Coptic and Islamic art (left); velvet coat with wide sleeves, Italian Renaissance style motif (right). (Countess Elsie Lee Gozzi, Venice)

The supplies of velvet were also running low. 'We have tried, and are still trying to obtain velvet, but I intend to continue using those materials with which, after a great deal of experimenting, I have obtained first-class results . . . I will try to avoid, right up until the last, doubtful experiments with materials of which I have had no experience.'[13] Yet as the trade war between England and Italy mounted, even the cotton became more difficult to obtain, and Mariano agreed to Elsie's suggestion that a new manufacturer be found in the United States.

In May 1936 Mariano and Henriette travelled to Greece for a change of scenery and in the hope of forgetting their problems for a while, 'since these last days have been anything but happy'.[14] Fortuny's photographs include an enchanting record of the places they visited and show him at sixty-five to be still remarkably youthful and energetic, but the trip itself offered only a short respite. By the summer the Orfei had run out of silk and no more Delphos robes could be produced. The situation was serious enough for him to sell an inherited collection of Goya drawings to the Metropolitan Museum in New York ('something I will regret all my life,' he wrote),[15]

Opposite: A funeral pall for the Duke of Lerma, assassinated in Madrid at the outbreak of the Spanish Civil War. The original cloth hangs in the Lerma Foundation in Toledo; a second version is in the Palazzo Fortuny. (Countess Elsie Lee Gozzi, Venice)

and for the first time he contemplated moving to Paris. Then in October, after eight months of correspondence and transatlantic 'phone calls, Elsie Lee brought good news. Thanks to her efforts and the intervention of the U.S. ambassador in Rome permission to import silk – though not velvet – was finally obtained.

As Mariano's personal affairs again took a turn for the better, a new situation arose which was profoundly disturbing to him in a very different way: the Spanish Civil War had broken out in July of that year, and his beloved countrymen were tearing each other apart. During the first months of the war the Duke of Lerma was assassinated in Madrid, and his widow commissioned a funeral pall from Fortuny, probably through Maria de Cardona. Mariano produced an enormous rectangular cloth, six metres by four, of black, silver and gold silk velvet with a great cross in the centre and the Lerma and Medinaceli family crests at the four corners. It was bounded by a wide border with foliar decorations and more crests; the effect was grandiose, and the seventeenth-century design and heraldic motifs gave the work a traditional look, an homage to his country's past. The great pall is now in the Lerma Foundation at the Tavera Hospital in Toledo.

By the mid 1930s the United States had become Fortuny's most important market. American women were wearing his clothes not only at home, but also in restaurants, at the theatre, for evenings in the country, and even on the most formal occasions. The Delphos gowns, the Scheherazades, the Grenadines, the velvet capes and jackets were admired and sought after by everyone from actresses and society ladies like Mrs Paul Mellon to the many young girls who dreamed of some day owning a Fortuny dress. In Mary McCarthy's novel *The Group* one of the characters commits suicide and her friends must decide how to dress the body. One of them, taking the initiative, buys an 'off-white silk pleated gown' on Madison Avenue: 'Then the others remembered that Kay had always longed for a Fortuny gown, which she never in her wildest dreams could have afforded.'[16] In reality Elsie Lee made great efforts to keep the clothes within a moderate price range. She even designed simple coats from Fortuny's cotton velvets to wear over the pleated dresses. Cotton velvet was subject to a lower import duty than silk velvet and thus much less expensive. The sketches and fabric samples were sent to Mariano for approval and she created a special department for selling them. Elsie's coats in no way pretended to be Fortuny models, but the fact that he allowed her to make them is a measure of the great confidence and esteem she enjoyed. In addition, Elsie began promoting Mariano's tempera paints, which could be bought individually or in the

Below and opposite: Two costumes designed by Fortuny for 'The Wedding Celebrations of Galeazzo Sforza and Bonne of Savoy', an historical pageant at the Castello Sforzesco in Milan in 1937. (Countess Elsie Lee Gozzi, Venice)

Arab with Hood. *Etching. c. 1938.*
The figure is taken from the painting
shown below. (Calcografía Nacional,
Madrid)

Below: The Nile at Luxor. *Tempera*
on canvas. Fortuny painted this during
his 1938 tour of Egypt with Henriette.
(Museo Fortuny, Venice)

Opposite: Fortuny in djellabah and
turban, late 1930s. He never lost his
love for dressing up. (Countess Elsie
Lee Gozzi, Venice)

artist's specially designed paintboxes. By 1937 she wrote to tell him that they were selling very well, and added: 'I hope the improvement in our business here will begin to reflect from your end so that at least you will not have any monetary worries.'[17]

The business in Europe was picking up as well. In the same year Mariano was approached by a Mrs Richter who wanted to open a Fortuny shop in London. His dresses and materials had long been popular with the British, but this shop was to be devoted exclusively to his merchandise. Mariano agreed to the idea on two conditions: first, that the cotton materials be used only for decoration and theatrical purposes, and, secondly, that no one else's clothes be sold together with his. Fortuny was unable to provide her with any silk dresses, however, as he was still unable to import the necessary raw material into Italy.

Mariano now became involved in a new project. The cleaning and restoration of the famous Tintorettos in Venice's Scuola Grande di San Rocco was completed in 1937, and after the paintings were rehung, it was decided that a new lighting system was needed for the room, which was very poorly lit. Fortuny was delighted with the commission to carry out the work. He was keenly interested in restoration and had himself done work on several important Tiepolos. In 1935, when he was very busy with his own exhibitions, he had somehow found time to be in Rome during the restoration of the Sistine Chapel, and while studying Michelangelo's work at close range had discovered nuances of colour that made him feel new respect for the craftsmanship of the great master. For the Tintorettos, Mariano employed the same principle of indirect lighting that he had invented for the theatre. The light was not shone directly onto the paintings, but reflected off a surface that diffused it; the effect was less harsh and the light gained a clarity and uniformity that was ideal for viewing the pictures. Henriette, writing to Elsie Lee, remarked: 'You can imagine his pleasure at having rescued from obscurity all those masterpieces that one will now see for the first time.'[18]

Once more, Fortuny turned his attention to the theatre, this time to assist in the staging of an historical pageant entitled *I Trionfi per le nozze di Galeazzo M. Sforza e Bonna di Savoia (The Wedding Celebrations of Galeazzo Sforza and Bonna of Savoy)* which took place on 9 June 1937 at the Sforza Castle in Milan with an enormous cast of both professional and amateur actors, including a number of Milanese aristocrats. His collaborators included two other well-known stage designers: Nicola Benois, son of Alexandre Benois who helped found the *Ballets Russes*, and Cito Filomarino

who had conceived the present spectacle. Mariano designed a magnificent series of costumes for the event, each one different from the others and each faithfully reflecting the character of the period being portrayed.

Fortuny had a quiet period in 1938, the year before war broke out again in Europe. After selling the Palazzo Martinengo, which had passed to him on María Luisa's death, he embarked on a grand tour of Egypt with Henriette. There he sketched the ruins of Karnak and Luxor, and painted a canvas entitled *The Nile at Luxor*. He became fascinated with the light in Egypt, and later added a new shade to his range of tempera colours, the luminous 'Egyptian blue'.

The advent of the Second World War meant, among other things, the blockade of Italy by the Allies, and the severing of Fortuny's links with America, Britain and the rest of the world. The Giudecca factory closed, all work ceased at the Palazzo Orfei, and Mariano took refuge in his studio, painting, studying and preparing new designs for the time when he could resume his normal activities. Peace was a long time in coming, however, and the ensuing years of scarcity and hardship seriously undermined his health. The *palazzo* was no longer heated throughout, and during one particularly chilly winter Mariano erected an Arab tent in the middle of the great hall where he could paint protected from the cold – it was, he told Countess Gozzi, very warm inside. At this time an artist's model came from Milan to sit for him, and he painted a number of nude portraits of a markedly erotic nature. He also spent a good deal of time taking photographs and cataloguing his various works.

Fortuny in his seventies in the mountains above Genoa, at Uscio. He frequently stayed there for rest and treatment for his asthma. (Countess Elsie Lee Gozzi, Venice)

The Giudecca factory was reopened after the war, but before production could be resumed repairs had to be made to the buildings whose walls had been damaged by the wartime sinking of an Italian battleship near the island. Fortuny re-established contact with the Lees and began filling orders for his cotton materials again, but on a much reduced scale. The market in America had changed, and he had to scale down his designs for the new high-rise apartment style of life. In Europe, with the Paris shop and other outlets gone, and the distribution network in shambles, it was necessary to rebuild the whole operation from scratch. However, Fortuny was no longer the young man he had been in the aftermath of the First World War when he seemed blessed with an inexhaustible supply of energy and new ideas. Past seventy, with the white hair and beard of a patriarch, he still seemed an imposing figure but his strength was waning.

Mariano went frequently to Uscio in the mountains above Genoa to rest and have his asthma treated, as he had done periodically over the years.

In Venice, he relied increasingly on Henriette and his faithful assistant Mario Beffagna to look after the day-to-day activities of the workshops and factory, and devoted much of his time to painting and reflection. He also began to seek the company of other artists again, particularly through his old 'club', the Order of the Valise, a light-hearted organization named after a discarded piece of luggage that had been discovered by one of its members. In truth, it was simply a group of old friends, Venetian landscape painters mostly, who liked to while away the afternoon at the Gorrizia restaurant talking about art. In 1947 Mariano's native country paid tribute to his talent when they made him a member of the Royal Academy of San Fernando in Madrid. Fortuny had entered a period of introspection and self-assessment. He returned once more to Wagner, preparing new sketches of the Ring cycle for sets at La Scala; he also painted a whole series of self-portraits, doing four almost identical pictures of himself in 1947 alone. He had analysed his own face in this way when, at eighteen, he had been on the verge of leaving the Palazzo Martinengo and his mother's world. Now, as if sensing that death was at hand, he prepared himself for a different departure.

Mariano's health took a sudden turn for the worse in 1948, when he was confined to bed for most of the year with severe abdominal pains. As a result of his illness he could no longer eat and began to lose weight rapidly; the condition was eventually diagnosed as intestinal cancer.

Henriette sent desperate cables to Elsie Lee in America asking for penicillin, which at the time was thought to cure almost any illness, and was difficult to obtain. Elsie responded immediately, mailing several parcels, but they were all stolen en route. Only one parcel, brought by a friend, ever reached Fortuny, and this could not save him. He died in the Palazzo Orfei on 2 May 1949.

Henriette, the young French model who had been treated like an outcast by Doña Cecilia and María Luisa when she first arrived in Venice, now found herself the sole heir to the Fortuny estate and the custodian of the hallowed family memories. Her marriage had produced no offspring and there were no children or grandchildren to whom she could pass on the tradition of the Palazzo Orfei, but the textiles, dresses and other objects which she had helped to create there were progeny of another kind, and they were destined to live on. In the years to come, Mariano Fortuny's canvases and etchings, his inventions and his contributions to the theatre would all pass into relative obscurity; only the work in silk and velvet, in cotton and other fabrics would endure, for these were his masterpieces, his finest paintings, and the truest expression of his genius.

VIII

REAPPRAISALS

In honour of Mr Fortuny the first design I put into production was called Spagnolo–*since he considered himself first and foremost a* Spaniard–*and the second* Granada *where he was born.*

COUNTESS ELSIE LEE GOZZI

One of four almost identical self-portraits painted by Fortuny shortly before his death. 1947. (Countess Elsie Lee Gozzi, Venice/Fototeca ASAC Biennale)

In the years following his death, little mention was made of Mariano Fortuny aside from one or two magazine pieces which were largely anecdotal and treated him as a mysterious, somewhat enigmatic figure. Henriette was shattered by the loss of her husband and unable to cope with the management of the Orfei and the Giudecca factory on her own. The *palazzo* workshops were closed, and although the shop on the ground floor continued to exist for some time, the remaining dresses, cushions and velvet capes lay around in a neglected state, gathering dust. Those who remembered Fortuny had long since bought his gowns and by now were likely to have stored them away in some attic; the new generation was unaware of him. Had it not been for Elsie Lee, Fortuny's work would quickly have been forgotten by his contemporaries and possibly lost for good.

Elsie was in New York when she heard of Mariano's death. She and her husband received the news as a personal tragedy and made preparations to leave as soon as possible for Venice, but on the eve of their departure Humphrey was killed in a car accident on Manhattan's Triboro Bridge. Suddenly the two men whom she loved and had worked so closely with over the years were gone. In the face of this double blow, Elsie responded with characteristic strength and determination. Following a short visit to her husband's family in England, she took the boat for Italy, going straight to the Palazzo Orfei to see what comfort she might give Henriette. Henriette was anxious for her to buy the factory, but for once Elsie was hesitant. 'Since I was in the same state as Madame Fortuny, I didn't know at first how I could manage both the American business and the Giudecca manufacturing

Mariano Fortuny
y Madrazo
1947

part. Giudecca was in such an obvious rundown condition.'[1] From the Orfei Elsie went on to her holiday villa at Forte dei Marmi, and here one day she found a tired, rather confused Henriette, who had undertaken the long journey from Venice by bus. She came with the conviction that her husband's work must continue, and she knew that Elsie was the only person who understood both the technical and commercial sides of the operation. 'It was this visit that persuaded me to go on with the work,'[2] recalls Countess Gozzi.

Elsie thereupon made arrangements to sell the villa and devoted her energies to the Giudecca enterprise, investing a considerable part of her own money in rebuilding the old factory. She repaired and modernized the buildings, refurbished the dwindling stock of raw materials, and totally reorganized the administration. With the help of Mario Beffagna and Angelina, another of Fortuny's old assistants, she resumed production of both the textiles and the Delphos gowns (which continued to be manufactured until

Below: Henriette in the Palazzo Fortuny, c. 1960.

Right: Dolores del Rio posing in a Delphos for Hollywood portrait photographer George Hurrell, c. 1941. (Countess Elsie Lee Gozzi, Venice/G. Hurrell)

Overleaf:
Left: Julie Christie photographed for British Vogue *on the Piazza San Marco, Venice, in a velvet cape and hood with Renaissance style motifs. Liselotte Höhs Collection. (Photograph by Castaldi © Condé Nast Publications Ltd.)*
Right: Julie Christie photographed for British Vogue *in the Palazzo Fortuny wearing pleated silk trousers and tunic of pleated silk. The pleated trousers were very rare and few have survived. (Liselotte Höhs, Venice. Photograph by Castaldi © Condé Nast Publications Ltd.)*

Opposite: Countess Gozzi in a Delphos and velvet coat, c. 1940. (Countess Elsie Lee Gozzi, Venice)

1952). At first she worked in cotton velvet, but the shortage and high cost of raw stock led her to concentrate entirely on pure cotton fabrics. In order to keep alive the memory of Fortuny, she also started a collection of objects, mementos and photographs recording his life. She became involved in every stage of the manufacturing process, personally mixing the paints and working over the material inch by inch as it underwent the successive operations. She began dividing her time equally between her American business and Venice, travelling to and fro by ocean liner. In the days before air travel, Elsie reckons to have made over a hundred such journeys: 'The *Conte Grande* and *Conte di Savoia* were fast ships – 6½ days to Genoa – and gave me an opportunity to rest, study, and decide what I wanted to work on when I arrived in Venice.'[3] She often made first proofs of a new design, and to this day practically every

length of material that is produced comes under her direct supervision. As the years went by Italy became her adopted country, and she eventually married a Venetian nobleman, Count Alvise Gozzi.

The Palazzo Orfei posed a different problem. It could not be dismantled nor did Henriette wish it to be, but in her grief and confusion following Mariano's death she came under the influence of several unscrupulous characters who encouraged her to make haphazard donations, and sell other items for a fraction of their true worth. It was during this period that the family collection of Hellenistic, Coptic and Hispano-Moresque textiles went to the Castello Sforzesco in Milan and the Venetian glass pieces went to the Murano Glass Museum.

Fortunately, Mariano de Madrazo appeared in Venice at this point to help Henriette settle her affairs. A cousin of Fortuny and one of his few surviving relatives, he arrived in time to recover a number of family heirlooms and prevent further dispersal of the *palazzo's* contents, suggesting instead the idea of setting up a Fortuny museum. He did propose, however, that certain paintings and drawings by Fortuny's father and Federico de Madrazo be donated to museums in Spain.

In 1951 Maria de Cardona went to Venice and succeeded in obtaining the collection of prints that Fortuny had made from his father's engraving plates. She divided this, donating part to the Calcografía Nacional (The National Collection of Etchings) and part to the Biblioteca Nacional (The

National Library), both in Madrid. The etchings, displayed in the same year at the Biblioteca Nacional, formed the second posthumous exhibition of Fortuny's work. The first occurred in the Spanish pavilion of the 1950 Venice Biennale, which put together a retrospective show of the two Fortunys and the Madrazo family: fourteen of Mariano's works were included, ranging from the early anatomical studies of 1890 to the last self-portrait painted in 1949.

In 1953 Henriette, carrying out Mariano's wishes, offered the Palazzo Orfei to the Spanish government, but was informed that they needed time to consider the proposal. A committee of architects and academics, set up to study the condition of the *palazzo*, produced two reports. The first provided for the restoration of the palace to its original state at the time of the Pesaro family; the second allowed for a partial restoration to ensure the survival of the building and its contents, and the installation of an academy for Spanish artists. A few intellectuals and journalists tried persuading the Spanish authorities to preserve the *palazzo* for the nation.[4] Maria de Cardona, who had worked tirelessly to promote Fortuny's work during his lifetime, began publishing articles and giving lectures to attract attention to the cause. Four years later the government finally reached a decision; the Ministry of Foreign Affairs thanked Henriette for her gracious offer, but said that they were unable to take it up for financial reasons. She then approached the Municipality of Venice, who accepted her gift with alacrity. The two conditions attached to the offer were first that Fortuny's vast studio should be preserved intact, and secondly that the remainder of the building be devoted to a cultural centre. Henriette herself continued to live in the Orfei until her death in 1965, surrounded by memories of Mariano and visited regularly by Elsie and Fortuny's young relative, Cecilia de Madrazo.

Because of Elsie Lee Gozzi's passionate interest in Fortuny, he became better known in America than in Europe. European museums did not begin to acquire his work until the mid 1960s, and there was little interest in him until the following decade, but in the United States museums had been collecting his dresses for many years. A major exhibition, organized by the designer Dorothy Jenkins with Elsie's help, took place in 1967 at Los Angeles County Museum. Fortuny's materials became popular again with museum designers who rediscovered their virtues in the decoration of large galleries. The Metropolitan Museum of New York, for example, which had a collection of Fortuny's dresses even during his lifetime, provided Elsie with several important commissions.

Lady Bonham Carter in a Fortuny dress purchased in Venice around 1920. (David Montgomery/Sunday Times, London)

Right: Tina Chow on the balcony of her London home with her collection of Fortuny dresses in her favourite garment, a silk cloak printed with the Bellini motif which appears on p. 144. (E. Momeñe)

Overleaf:
Left: Delphos with a short tunic photographed by Cecil Beaton. (Victoria and Albert Museum, London)
Right: Geraldine Chaplin during the making of her husband's film Mama Cumple 100 Años *in 1979. The Delphos and silk gauze wrap belonged to her mother Oona Chaplin. (Courtesy of Geraldine Chaplin)*

By the early 1960s the first collectors had begun to appear, young women like Liselotte Höhs. The wife of Henriette's last solicitor, Höhs went to the Palazzo Orfei in 1958, and seeing for the first time the Delphos, the *jacquettes persanes*, the *casaquins persans*, and the printed velvets, began to acquire all she could. In America there were others – Oona Chaplin, Gloria Vanderbilt and Evelyn Avedon – who began to make an impact with their private collections, and in 1962 the New York *Herald Tribune* wrote of the many women who were 'making a cult of collecting the pleated Fortuny dresses'.[5] The quality of his clothes fascinated many of the famous *couturiers* of the 1960s and 1970s. Some like Balenciaga were enthusiastic admirers of Fortuny without being directly influenced by him, but others, such as the American designer Mary McFadden or Karl Lagerfeld of Chloe, were deeply affected at some point in their careers. Lagerfeld copied the Delphos gowns for his own collection in 1975 when he declared, 'For me the most beautiful dresses have always been the ancient draped models, which preserve the fabrics in their original state and in which the material is not altered.'[6]

During the latter part of the 1970s there occurred what one could almost call a Fortuny revival. If in the 1960s Edwardian dresses were rediscovered by the younger generation, in the 1970s their interest became focused on the 1920s – Fortuny's era – and his gowns began appearing regularly in motion pictures, on television, and in the fashion magazines. Julie Christie, Lauren Hutton and Marisa Berenson are but a few of the personalities who were photographed in them. Grandmothers, remembering the Fortuny dresses they had abandoned in old trunks, brought them out again for the new generation to wear, and they could be seen again on well-dressed women at theatre openings, the opera and other formal events. Consequently the London night-club Annabel's organized a fashion show devoted exclusively to Fortuny's clothes which a number of collectors had lent for the occasion. His materials also began to gain widespread publicity, as illustrated by a contemporary film of the Italian director Liliana Cavani, *Beyond Good and Evil*, in which they were used for several scenes.

Thirty years after his death, Mariano Fortuny had become a figure of historical interest. Any serious exhibition dealing with fashion in the early part of the twentieth century had to include at least one Delphos gown and as a result his dresses commanded increasingly high prices whenever they appeared at auction: Christie's achieved the world record for a Delphos when it sold one in May 1979 for 3500 dollars. In Lyon, the centre of the French textile industry which for years provided Fortuny with his velvets, technical experts[7] began examining his methods of working but were still unable to

Violet silk Delphos from the collection of Gloria Vanderbilt. (Photograph by Richard Avedon)

discover how he achieved some of his remarkable results. They said he used a mixture of different techniques on the same length of fabric – blocking, stencils, brush – in a manner that is very difficult to determine. It had been thought that he used actual gold and silver when printing his fabrics, but laboratory tests have shown that the silver effects were quite simply achieved

with aluminium and the gold effects with bronze. This is not an uncommon procedure for textile printers, but surprising in the light of the exceptional quality of Fortuny's fabrics. These investigations were part of the preparations for one of the largest exhibitions of his work ever assembled. Lasting over two years, and travelling from France to England and then on to the United States, the exhibition opened in the spring of 1980 at the Musée Historique des Tissus in Lyon. The show was designed to cover all aspects of Fortuny's life and work and to pay tribute to his various skills as a designer, artist and inventor, presenting his art in the wider context of the special world in which it was born.

In the final analysis, Fortuny's paintings and engravings, his *objets d'art*, his innovations in lighting and stage design, his dresses and textiles, and his numerous inventions were all part of a single grand theatrical production in which he assumed all the roles. 'Art is my life's aim' he declared as a young man, but in fact the converse is also true: he made his own life a work of art. In this sense the artist himself is perhaps the most compelling feature of his world. In an age of increasing specialization, when one is encouraged to know more and more about less and less, Fortuny stands out as an example not only of what a man can do, but more importantly of what he can be.

APPENDIX

This short list of Fortuny models, while in no way complete, attempts to offer a methodical approach to the artist's work as a dress designer. For the purpose of comparison, the clothing has been divided into basic categories, but even these cannot be interpreted as a formal classification for there is no clear distinction between the groups, and they necessarily overlap. Fortuny worked with a few simple ideas and shapes from which he developed countless variations, never creating the same garment twice.

THE DELPHOS

The Delphos, a long gown of pleated silk, existed in many different versions and in every imaginable shade of colour. It was Fortuny's most popular creation, which he started producing in about 1907 and continued until his death in 1949.

1. Pleated and undulated silk dress shown with Knossos scarf. (Museo Fortuny, Venice)

2. Early model with cords at the back which made it cling to the body. (Museo Fortuny, Venice)

3. Dress with batwing sleeves. (Countess Elsie Lee Gozzi, Venice)

4. Sleeveless dress; the most popular version of the Delphos. (Christie's East, New York)

5. Dress with long sleeves. (Neil Dorr)

6. Dress with crossed straps over bodice.

7. Dress with short tunic hanging in points at the side; batwing sleeves. (Maurice Beck and Macgregor © The Condé Nast Publications Ltd.)

8. Sleeveless dress with short tunic hanging at the front, back and sides. (Victoria and Albert Museum, London)

9. Black dress and matching belt with fleur-de-lys motif stencilled in gold. (Museo Fortuny, Venice)

LONG GOWNS

Aside from the Delphos there were three basic types of silk or velvet gown: the velvet-panelled kind of medieval and Renaissance inspiration; that which hung freely from the shoulders; and 'Directoire' models adjusted under the bosom by a cord or belt.

1. Velvet gown stencilled in gold Lucca motif; pleated silk insets at sides and sleeves. (Costume Council Fund, Los Angeles County Museum of Art)

2. Side view of velvet panelled dress showing insets of pleated silk. (Countess Elsie Lee Gozzi, Venice)

3. Velvet gown with Italian Renaissance style motif. (The Fine Arts Museum of San Francisco)

4. Silk gown with imitation lace motif. (Museo Fortuny, Venice)

5. Silk gown similar in shape to Coptic tunics. Motifs inspired by Coptic textiles. (Museo Fortuny, Venice)

6. Silk gown. Motifs inspired by Arab, Coptic and Persian designs. (Museo Fortuny, Venice)

7. Silk gown decorated with fur at hem and cuffs. Motifs based on Coptic textiles. (Museo Fortuny, Venice)

8. 'Directoire' gown. Motifs from Jacopo Bellini's sketchbook of textile designs in the Louvre. (Museo Fortuny, Venice)

9. 'Directoire' gown. Motifs inspired by 16th century textiles. (Museo Fortuny, Venice)

10. 'Directoire' gown. Silk gauze. Imitation lace motif. (Museo Fortuny, Venice)

11. 'Directoire' gown. Velvet and silk gauze. Lace motif of early 17th century inspiration. (Museo Fortuny, Venice)

12. 'Directoire' gown. Silk. Motifs inspired by Cretan art. (Museo Fortuny, Venice)

SILK OVER-GARMENTS

The very light silk garments worn over the dresses were conceived more as ornaments than as protective clothing. These included tunics, capes, jackets, wraps and coats of varying lengths.

1. Silk gauze tunic over Delphos. Lace motif inspired by Persian textiles. Venetian glass beads along border. (Museo Fortuny, Venice)

2. Silk gauze tunic over
Delphos. Renaissance style
motif along border.
(Courtesy of Amanda
Palmer)

3. Loose fitting tunic over
Delphos. Near Eastern
style motif. (Museo
Fortuny, Venice)

4. Short cape in silk gauze.
Imitation lace motif.
Venetian glass beads along
lower border. (Museo
Fortuny, Venice)

5. Short jacket printed in gold
and silver. Islamic inspired
motif. (Countess Elsie Lee
Gozzi, Venice)

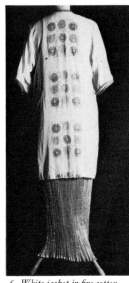

6. White jacket in fine cotton
toile. Blue and gold Persian
inspired motifs. (Liselotte
Höhs, Venice/E. Momeñe)

7. Long black vest in silk
gauze. Gold Persian inspired
motifs. (Tina Chow
Collection/E. Momeñe)

8. Long coat in silk gauze.
Venetian glass beads along
lower border. Printed silk
piping at openings and sleeves.
(Museo Fortuny, Venice)

9. Three-quarter wrap cut in a
square with openings for the
head and arms. Cretan
inspired motifs. (Museo
Fortuny, Venice)

10. Long wrap with fur lining
at collar and sleeves. Motifs
inspired by Persian textiles.
(Museo Fortuny, Venice)

11. Long coat with very wide
sleeves. Motifs inspired by
Coptic art. (Museo Fortuny
Venice)

12. Long red coat with wide
sleeves. Motifs inspired by
Coptic art. (Tina Chow
Collection)

13. Long coat. Shape and motifs
inspired by Persian and
Turkish costumes. Rare
example. (Museo Fortuny,
Venice)

VELVET OVER-GARMENTS

The velvet jackets, wraps, capes
and coats were produced on a
larger scale than the silk over-
garments and were more popular.

1. Short velvet tunic jacket. Floral motif inspired by Persian
textiles. Stencilled in silver. (Gift of the Estate of
Mrs Stanley R. McCormick/Los Angeles County Museum of Art)

2. *Short velvet jacket. Black with Persian inspired motifs in gilded metal. (Crown copyright/Victoria and Albert Museum, London)*

3. *Three-quarter coat. Dark brown velvet. Persian inspired motif. Stencilled in silver. (Countess Elsie Lee Gozzi, Venice)*

4. *Three-quarter coat. Persian style motif. (Countess Elsie Lee Gozzi, Venice)*

5. *Three-quarter coat with belt. Shape and motifs of Persian inspiration. (Courtesy of Amanda Palmer)*

6. *Three-quarter coat. Motifs based on 14th century Lucca textiles. (Courtesy* VOGUE, *Copyright © 1923, 1951 by Condé Nast Publications Inc.)*

7. *Group of long coats inspired by ceremonial robes of Venetian Doges. (Museo Fortuny, Venice)*

8. *Long coat. Pomegranate motif of Renaissance inspiration. (Museo Fortuny, Venice)*

9. *Long coat. Motifs inspired by Persian and Turkish textiles. (Museo Fortuny, Venice)*

10. *Short cape with hood, buttons and cord. Printed with stripes, and Coptic inspired motif stencilled in silver. (Countess Elsie Lee Gozzi, Venice)*

THEATRICAL COSTUMES AND ECCLESIASTICAL VESTMENTS

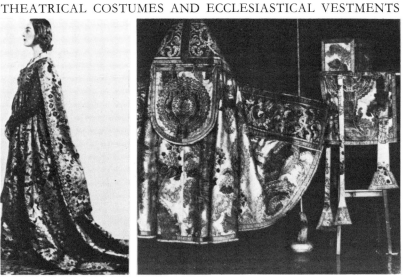

11. *Long cape with hood. Light brown velvet with stripes. (Countess Elsie Lee Gozzi, Venice)*

1. *Velvet costume stencilled in gold, for an historical pageant set in the 16th century. (Countess Elsie Lee Gozzi, Venice)*

2. *Ecclesiastical vestments and accessories. Velvet with motifs based on Renaissance and 16th century textiles. (Museo Fortuny, Venice/E. Momeñe)*

3. *Dalmatic. Velvet with motifs inspired by 16th century textiles. (Museo Fortuny, Venice/E. Momeñe)*

Patents Registered by Fortuny

All these inventions were patented in the Office National de la Propriété Industrielle in Paris.

1. Système d'éclairage scénique pour lumière indirecte. No. 309.588. 2 April 1901.
2. Système de coloration, décoration et graduation par lumière indirecte naturelle ou artificielle. Addition to No. 309.588. 26 April 1901.
3. Appareil de décoration théâtrale. No. 329.176. 7 February 1903.
4. Système d'éclairage en lumière diffuse. No. 339.140. 31 October 1903.
5. Système de constitution d'une paroi concave au moyen d'une capacité gouflable. No. 341.952. 6 April 1904.
6. Lampe à arc. No. 359.530. 25 January 1905.
7. Système d'éclairage mixte. No. 360.627. 3 March 1905.
8. Système d'éclairage en lumière diffuse. No. 5.597. Addition to No. 339.140. 6 March 1905.
9. Système de constitution d'une paroi concave au moyen d'une capacité gouflable. No. 4.676. Addition to No. 341.952. 6 April 1905.
10. Système de transmission asservie. No. 372.242. 14 February 1906.
11. Système pour obtenir la variation de l'intensité des lampes à arc. No. 376.679. 19 June 1906.
12. Système d'éclairage scénique par lumière indirecte. No. 7.714. Addition to No. 309.588. 14 May 1907.
13. Genre d'étoffe plissée-ondulée. No. 414.119. 10 June 1909.
14. Procédé d'impression polychrome sur tissus, papiers, etc. No. 419.269. 21 October 1909.
15. Genre de vêtement pour femmes. No. 408.629. 4 November 1909.
16. Système de support. No. 415.622. 4 May 1910.
17. Procédé d'impression sur tissus, papiers, etc. No. 427.307. 24 May 1910.
18. Système de propulsion des navires. No. 449.715. 30 December 1911.
19. Dispositif de théâtre. No. 629.456. 5 May 1926.
20. Dispositif permettant de faire varier progressivement l'intensité des sources lumineuses. No. 694.028. 16 April 1930.
21. Papier photographique. No. 728.962. 3 March 1931.
22. Rideau transparent, flexible et pliable pour vitrines, bibliothèques, armoires et meubles analogues. No. 763.964. 16 November 1933.

Notes

Chapter I: THE FORMATIVE YEARS
(1) Angela Mariutti de Sanchez Rivero, *Quattro Spagnoli a Venezia*, Venice, 1957, p.132.
(2) Quoted by Baron Charles de Davillier in his introduction to the sales catalogue of Mariano Fortuny y Marsal's works at the Hotel Drouot, Paris, 26–30 April 1875.
(3) Edouard de Beaumont wrote: 'This desire to restore the purity of their original form to certain helmets and pieces of harness, led him, quite naturally, to do research and to attempt some of the old manufacturing processes, which in days gone by were barely revealed even by the metal-workers to the merchants.' *Ibid.*, pp. 73–4.
(4) Corrado Tumiati, 'Il mio vicino mago', *Corriere della Sera*, 6 Sept 1932.
(5) Ugo Ojetti, *Cose viste*, Milan, 1925, p.138.
(6) *Ibid.*, p.141.
(7) Marcel Proust, *La Prisonnière* in *A la Recherche du Temps Perdu*, edited by Pierre Clarac and André Ferré, Paris, 1954, Vol III, p.369.

Chapter II: VENICE: PAINTING, DRAWING, ENGRAVING
(1) Henri de Régnier, *L'Altana ou la Vie Venitienne, 1899–1924*, Paris, 1927, Vol. I, p.55.
(2) Philippe Jullian, *Dreamers of Decadence*, London, 1971, p.143.
(3) Gino Damerini, 'D'Annunzio a Venezia', *Quaderni D'Annunziani*, Vol. V, 1943, p.54.
(4) Angelo Conti, *La Beata Riva, trattato dell'oblio* (The Blessed Bank, a Treatise on Oblivion), Milan, 1900. Written as a result of a discourse by D'Annunzio.
(5) Unpublished letter to her brother Ricardo.
(6) Sickert made this comment in a letter to his friend, the French painter and writer Jacques-Emile Blanche. Published by the latter in his book of memoirs, *Portrait of a Lifetime, 1870–1914*, London, 1937, pp.46–7.
(7) Recounted to the author by Mariano de Madrazo, Fortuny's first cousin.
(8) Quoted in Lilian Browse, *Sickert*, London, 1960, p.26.
(9) Recounted in a letter by Doña Cecilia to her brother Ricardo.
(10) Quoted from Sara Stevenson and Helen Bennet, *Van Dyck in Check Trousers: Fancy Dress in Art and Life, 1700–1900*, Trustees of the National Gallery of Scotland, 1978, p.2.
(11) Vittorio Pica, 'L'arte mondiale alla III Esposizione di Venezia nel 1899', *Emporium*, Special Issue, 1899, p.74.
(12) Achille de Carlo, *L'Arte a Venezia*, Padua, 1899.
(13) From Fortuny's notes of 10 Nov 1896, quoted in Mariutti de Sanchez Rivero, *op. cit.*, p.140.

(14) The manufacture of Fortuny tempera is more fully described in Chapter VII. See René Piot, *Les Tempera Vénitiennes de Mariano Fortuny*, a leaflet published in Venice in 1933.
(15) Mariutti de Sanchez Rivero, *op. cit.*, p.139.
(16) Titian women with long, wavy hair can be seen in paintings such as the *Woman in Front of a Mirror* in the National Gallery, Washington, the *Venus Anadiomeda* in the Scottish National Gallery, Edinburgh, and the *Flora* in the Uffizi Gallery in Florence.
(17) Rogelio de Egusquiza (1845–1915) had met Mariano's father in Paris and Rome. He felt unfulfilled by the sort of frivolous and superficial painting he was doing at the time and his search for a deeper and more spiritual reality led to his discovering Wagner and Schopenhauer. In 1879 he paid his first visit to Bayreuth. Wagner made such an impression on him that his whole life and artistic output changed. Henceforth Egusquiza was to lead an extremely austere life, dedicated almost exclusively to the portrayal of Wagnerian iconography. See Aureliano de Beruete, *Rogelio de Egusquiza*, Madrid, 1918. Josephin Sar Peladan, who founded the 'Catholic Rose Croix of the Temple and the Grail' and who was very influential with Symbolists and Decadents, wrote of him: 'Monsieur de Egusquiza alone has understood how Wagner and his *leitmotiven* could carry on Delacroix's passionate art. One day he will unveil the astonishing fruit of his mysterious labours. His vocation as a great painter was determined at Bayreuth, as was my genius as a tragedian.' Quoted in Jullian, *op. cit.*, pp.65–6.
(18) Quoted in Mariutti de Sanchez Rivero, *op. cit.*, pp.135–6.
(19) *Ibid.*, p.140.

Chapter III: STAGE-LIGHTING AND THEATRICAL DESIGN
(1) Tumiati, *op. cit.*
(2) Ferruccio Marotti, *Amleto o dell'oxymoron, Studi e note sull' estetica della scena moderna*, Rome, 1966, pp.18–19.
(3) Adolphe Appia, *La Musique et la Mise en Scène (1892–1897)*, Bern, 1963, p.55.
(4) Mariano Fortuny, *Eclairage Scénique: Système Fortuny*, Paris, 1904, p.10. A small 13-page booklet describing his new lighting system.
(5) *Ibid.*, pp.1–2.
(6) *Ibid.*, p.3.
(7) He patented it in Paris on 2 April 1901, calling it '*Système d'éclairage scénique par lumière indirecte*'. On 26 April he added an improvement to the original system and decided to change its name to '*Système de coloration, décoration et gradation par lumière indirecte naturelle et arti-*

ficielle'. Many additions and improvements were added during the following years.

(8) Fortuny, *op. cit.*, pp.8–9.

(9) *Ibid.*, p.3.

(10) *Ibid.*, p.7.

(11) *Ibid.*, p.13.

(12) From Wagner's libretti published by Schott & Co. Ltd in London.

(13) Damerini, *op. cit.*, p.90.

(14) Giannino Omero Gallo, 'La casa magica di San Benedetto'. A cutting of the newspaper in which this article was published was given to the author by Cecilia de Madrazo, Mariano's first cousin. Neither the name of the newspaper nor the date the article was published are known.

(15) Cronachetta Artistica, 'Gli scenari del Tristano et Isota', *Emporium*, Vol. XIII, No. 73, Jan 1901. The review is signed V.P., possibly Vittorio Pica.

(16) Feder, 'Gli scenari del Tristano e Isotta alla Scala', *La Lettura*, Vol. I, Jan 1901.

(17) Gino Damerini, journalist and expert on D'Annunzio, wrote an extensive article entitled 'Ricordi su Eleonora Duse e Gabriele D'Annunzio' (published in *Quaderni D'Annunziani*, Vols XII–XIII, 1958) describing this collaboration. In it he published some of the letters D'Annunzio wrote to Fortuny. These had first been published by Giannino Omero Gallo in *Il Roma della Domenica* in 1937. For the relationship between Fortuny and D'Annunzio, see also Damerini's 'D'Annunzio a Venezia', *Quaderni D'Annunziani*, Vol. V, 1943.

(18) In Damerini's 'Ricordi', pp.92 and 93.

(19) Quoted from Marotti, *op. cit.*, p.91. For contacts between Fortuny and Appia see also *ibid.*, pp.89 and 90.

(20) Hermann, Graf von Keyserling, 'Die erste Bewirklichung von Appias Ideen zur Reform der Bühne', supplement to the *Allgemeine Zeitung*, 6 April 1903.

(21) Ch.-M. Widor, 'Nouveau Système d'Eclairage de la Scène', *Le Menestrel*, Paris, 15 April 1906, p.117.

(22) *Ibid.*, p.117.

(23) Quoted from María de Cardona, 'Mariano Fortuny y Madrazo', *Arte Español*, Jan–April 1950, p.36.

(24) This information was kindly provided by Dr Heinrich Hüesmann, Director of the Theatre Museum of Munich, who is preparing an important work on Reinhardt. In a letter dated 5 February 1979 he writes: 'There is a letter from Max Reinhardt, Sils Maria, to Berthold Hein, Berlin, written on the 28th of July 1905, telling of a special "Himmelskuppel" (sky vault) which Reinhardt had seen in Paris.'

(25) In Germany the theatres of Berlin, Dresden, Königsberg, Wiesbaden, Karlsruhe, Stuttgart and Duisburg were equipped with Fortuny's system.

Chapter IV: FASHION AND TEXTILES

(1) Henri de Régnier, *op. cit.*, Vol. I, p.167.

(2) Philippe Jullian, *D'Annunzio*, London, 1972, p.161.

(3) Quoted from Allen Staley, *Post Pre-Raphaelitism in Victorian High Renaissance*, exhibition catalogue, Manchester (City Art Gallery), Minneapolis (The Minneapolis Institute of Art), New York (The Brooklyn Museum), 1878–9, pp.24 and 25.

(4) *Ibid.*

(5) *Ibid.*

(6) Walter Crane, *Ideals in Art*, London, 1905, p.178.

(7) Vern G. Swanson, *Sir Lawrence Alma Tadema*, London, 1977, p.28.

(8) Quoted from *Liberty's 1875–1975*, exhibition catalogue, Victoria & Albert Museum, London, 1975, p.11.

(9) Crane, *op. cit.*, pp.175–6.

(10) Lady Diana Cooper, *The Rainbow Comes and Goes*, London, 1958, p.60.

(11) V. Svetlov (in collaboration with L. Bakst), *Le Ballet contemporain*, Paris, 1912, p.32.

(12) *Ibid.*, p.22.

(13) Office National de la Propriété Industrielle, Paris, *Genre de Vêtement pour femmes*, Brevet d'Invention No. 408.629. Submitted 4 Nov. 1909.

(14) *Genre d'Etoffe plissée-ondulée*, Brevet d'Invention No. 414.119. Submitted 10 June 1909.

(15) Marcel Proust, *A la Recherche du Temps Perdu, La Prisonnière*, Vol. III, p.368. All the quotations from Proust are from the French edition, edited by Pierre Clarac and André Ferré, published in 3 volumes by La Pleiade in 1954. The English translation is from Scott-Moncrieff's edition, London, 1957.

(16) *Ibid.*, p.368.

(17) Office National de la Propriété Industrielle, Paris, *Procédé d'impression polychrome sur tissus, papier, etc.*, Brevet d'Invention No. 419.269, submitted 11 Oct 1909.

(18) Fortuny described the *katagami* as follows: 'It consists of a drawing cut out of two suitable sheets of paper which are then glued together. Pressed between them are hairs of filaments meant to bind or unite the different parts of the drawing.' Office National de la Propriété Industrielle, Paris, *Procédé d'impression sur tissus, papiers, etc.*, Brevet d'Invention No. 427.307, submitted 24 May 1910.

(19) *Ibid.*

(20) *Ibid.*

(21) Proust, *op. cit.*, Vol. III, p.368.

Chapter V: FORTUNY AND THE WORLD

(1) From a *Vogue* magazine of the period. Quoted in Palmer White's *Poiret*, London, 1973, p.35.

(2) In the Rome edition of 1932, p.282.

(3) Lady Diana Cooper, *op. cit.*, p.61.

(4) From a letter to Maria Hahn dated 18 Feb 1916, published in the catalogue of the Marcel Proust exhibition at the

Whitworth Art Gallery, Manchester in 1956. No. 85, p.24.

(5) Proust, *op. cit.*, Vol. III, p.399.

(6) See Emile Henriot, 'Deshabillés' in *Gazette du Bon Ton*, Dec 1912 and *Secrets d'Elégance*, catalogue of the exhibition organized by the Musée de la Mode et du Costume in Paris, 1978–9.

(7) See Felix Poppenberg, 'Dekorative Variationen' in *Der Türmer*, 1907–8, pp.741–2.

(8) See Arnold Haskell, *Diaghilev, His Artistic and Private Life*, London, 1935, pp.184, 185, 190; Prince Peter Lieven, *The Birth of Ballets-Russes*, London, 1956, p.71; Svetlov, *Le Ballet contemporain*, Paris, 1912, p.35 *et seq.*

(9) Proust, *op. cit.*, Vol. III, p.369.

(10) This information comes from Denise Poiret, the couturier's widow.

(11) This tunic was given to the Union Française des Arts du Costume by its owner Mme le Bas, who remembered having bought it at Poiret's. It has been exhibited as No. 57f in *Marcel Proust et Son Temps*, 1971, at the Musée Jacquemart-André in Paris, and as No. 74 in *Paul Poiret*, 1976, at the New York Fashion Institute of Technology.

(12) Whitney, *op. cit.*, p.40.

(13) *Ibid.*, p.21.

(14) *Vogue* (London), 'Ancient Art meets modern Fashion half-way', 15 Oct 1916.

(15) Gino Damerini, 'Ricordi su Eleonora Duse e Gabriele d'Annunzio', *Quaderni D'Annunziani*, Vol. XII–XIII, 1958, p.161.

(16) D'Annunzio was to write again to Fortuny in his usual passionate style to attract his attention. 'Oh wicked Mariano, aren't you ashamed at having abandoned and forgotten your faithful companion in art? Where can I come to inflict the punishment you deserve? And yet I so loved and admired you, as you loved me, in the early days of the Orfei. I embrace you with strangling force. Yours forever, Gabriele D'Annunzio.' Damerini, *op. cit.*, p.180.

Chapter VI: THE TWENTIES

(1) As stated in a letter from Countess Gozzi, New York, 14 February 1979.

(2) 'Mariano Fortuny', in *La Renaissance de l'Art Français et des Industries de luxe*, June 1924, p.312 *et seq.*

(3) *Vogue* (New York), 'The Beauty of Fortuny is brought to America', 15 May 1923.

(4) Catalogue of the 1925 Exposition des Arts Decoratifs et Industriels, Paris, Vol. IX, *La Parure*, pp.11, 12.

(5) Celia Haddon, 'Enduring Fashion', *Sunday Times Magazine*, London, 1 March 1976.

(6) Like the palace of the Marques de Lema which later passed to the Luca de Tena family and the palace of the dukes de Medinaceli.

(7) Ojetti, *op. cit.*, p.141.

(8) *Ibid.*, p.141.

(9) The idea for this theatre was also patented. Office National de la Propriété Industrielle, Paris, *Dispositif de théâtre*, Brevet d'Invention No. 629.456, submitted 5 May 1926.

(10) Alberto de Angelis, *Scenografi italiani de ieri et di oggi*, Rome, 1938, p.109.

(11) Alberto Spaini, 'Mariano Fortuny', *L'Italia Letteraria*, 29 July 1929.

(12) Corrado Pavolcini, 'Per un teatro di domani', in *Storia del teatro italiano* edited by Silvio D'Amico, Milan, 1936. p.366.

(13) Spaini, *op. cit.*

Chapter VII: THE FINAL YEARS

(1) From an unpublished letter to Humphrey Lee from Fortuny, Milan, 10 Dec 1933.

(2) From a letter to Humphrey Lee, 21 May 1934.

(3) *Ibid.*

(4) From a letter to the author in 1979.

(5) Office National de la Propriété Industrielle, Paris, *Papier photographique*, Brevet d'Invention No. 728.962, submitted 3 March 1931.

(6) René Piot, *Les Tempera Fortuny*, pp.3–5.

(7) *Ibid.*, p.1.

(8) Zamaçois wrote the text for the Parisian exhibition, which was later used for the Milan exhibition.

(9) From a letter to Elsie McNeill Lee, Venice, 14 Feb 1936.

(10) Giannino Omero Gallo, 'La casa magica di San Benedetto'. See Chapter III, note 14.

(11) From a letter to Elsie Lee, Venice, 14 Feb 1936.

(12) *Ibid.*

(13) From a letter to Elsie Lee, Venice, 12 May 1936.

(14) *Ibid.*

(15) From a letter to Elsie Lee, Venice, 14 Feb 1936.

(16) Mary McCarthy, *The Group*, Penguin Books, 1970.

(17) From a letter to Henriette Fortuny from Elsie Lee, New York, 9 Feb 1937.

(18) From a letter to Elsie Lee from Henriette, Venice, 27 Feb 1937.

Chapter VIII: REAPPRAISALS

(1) From a letter to the author, Nov 1979.

(2) *Ibid.*

(3) *Ibid.*

(4) Like Julian Cortes Cavanillas, who wrote an article praising Fortuny in the influential Madrid newspaper *ABC* entitled 'Recuerde España a Mariano Fortuny'.

(5) Eugenia Sheppard, 'The Fortuny Dress', *Herald Tribune*, 10 Sept 1962.

(6) The statement appeared in French *Vogue*, April 1975, in an article about the revival of Neo-classicism in that year's fashion. Lagerfield versions of the Delphos are illustrated in English *Vogue*, 1 Oct 1975.

(7) M. Gabriel Vial and Mlle Odile Valansot.

Museums Containing Fortuny Exhibits

England
BATH, Museum of Costume; LONDON, Victoria & Albert Museum (important collection of garments and textiles)

France
PARIS, Palais Galliera, Musée de la Mode et du Costume (important collection of garments); PARIS, Union Française des Arts du Costume

Italy
FLORENCE, Galleria degli Uffizi; MILAN, Teatro alla Scala; VENICE, Ca Pesaro, Museo d'Arte Moderna; VENICE, Fondazione Giorgio Cini (some rare pieces that belonged to Eleonora Duse); VENICE, Palazzo Fortuny (the artist's house, partly untouched – important collection of paintings, engravings, photographs, dresses, textiles, theatrical sketches, stage models, mechanical devices, personal memorabilia)

Japan
KYOTO, Costume Institute

Northern Ireland
BELFAST, Ulster Museum

Scotland
EDINBURGH, The Royal Scottish Museum; GLASGOW, Glasgow Museums and Art Galleries

Spain
MADRID, Biblioteca Nacional (important collection of drawings and engravings; MADRID, Calcografía Nacional in the Real Academia de Bellas Artes de S. Fernando (important collection of engravings and copper plates bequeathed by Fortuny's widow); MADRID, Museo Español de Arte Contemporaneo; REUS, Colegiata de Reus; TOLEDO, Fundación Lerma

U.S.A.
ALLENTOWN, Penn., Museum of Art; BOSTON, Mass., Museum of Fine Arts; CLEVELAND, Ohio, Cleveland Museum of Art; HARTFORD, Conn., Wadsworth Atheneum; LOS ANGELES, Ca., Los Angeles County Museum (important collection of garments and textiles); NEWARK, N.J., Newark Museum; NEW YORK, Brooklyn Museum (important collection of garments); NEW YORK, Cooper-Hewitt Museum; NEW YORK, Fashion Institute of Technology; NEW YORK, Metropolitan Museum of Art (very important collection of garments; some textiles); NEW YORK, Museum of the City of New York; PHILADELPHIA, Pa., Philadelphia Museum of Art; PHOENIX, Az., Phoenix Museum of Art; PROVIDENCE, R.I., Rhode Island School of Design; SAN ANTONIO, Tex., San Antonio Museum Association; SAN FRANCISCO, Ca., Fine Arts Museum of San Francisco; WASHINGTON, D.C., Smithsonian Institution

Select Bibliography

Adami, Giuseppe. *Un secolo di scenografia alla Scala*. Milan, 1945

Alegre Nuñez, Luis. *Catalogo de la Calcografia Nacional*. Madrid, 1968

Angelis, Alberto de. *Scenografi italiani di ieri e di oggi*. Rome, 1938

Antona-Traversi, C. *Gabriele D'Annunzio, Curriculum Vitae*. 2 vols. Rome, 1932

Anonymous
—'La Coupole–Décor Fortuny du théâtre de la Scala à Milan' in *Le Genie Civil*, Vol. LXXX, No. 20, 20 May 1922
—'The Beauty of Fortuny is brought to America' in *Vogue* (New York), 15 May 1923
—'Mariano Fortuny' in *La Renaissance de l'Art Français et des Industries de luxe*, No. 6, June 1924
—'Calendario y lunario, la vida breve' in *Blanco y Negro*, 3 May 1925
—'Old brocades by the reel' in the *Graphic*, 3 July 1926
—'Our lives from day to day' in *Vogue* (London), 21 Sept 1927
—'Fortuny of Venice' in the *Nomad*, April 1928
—*Cupole Fortuny per scenografia teatrale della S.A. Leonardo da Vinci*. Milan, 1931
—'Cronica de la Academia: donacion de aguafuertes de los 2 Fortuny' in *Boletin de la Academia de San Fernando*, 1955–7
—'Kore sculpture in cloth: Mrs Wyatt Emory Cooper in her fabled Fortuny dresses, photographed by Avedon' in *Vogue* (New York), Dec 1969
—'Cecil Beaton's own gallery of fashion' in *Vogue* (London), 1 Oct 1971
—'Julie Christie in Venice: her dress is her Fortuny' in *Vogue* (London), July 1973
—'The compleat Chloe' in *Vogue* (London, 1 Oct 1974

Battersby, Martin. *The Decorative Twenties*. London, 1969

Baxter, Leonora R. 'History portrayed in fabrics' in the *Golden Book*, May 1934

Blanche, Jacques-Emile. *Portraits of a lifetime, 1870–1914*. London, 1937

Blasi, Bruno. 'Con la firma di Fortuny' in *Panorama*, 22 Aug 1978

Bracchi, Luigi. 'Venezia città surreale' in *Il Giornale dell' Arte*, 15 Oct, 1 Nov, 1946

Browse, Lilian. *Sickert*. London, 1960

Cardona, Maria de. 'Mariano Fortuny y Madrazo' in *Arte Español*, Jan–April 1950

Cardona, Maria de. 'Rapsodia fortuniana' in *Gran Mundo*, No. 3, 1951

Cardona, Maria de. 'Exposicion Fortuny y Madrazo en la Biblioteca Nacional' in *Revista de Archivos Bibliotecas y Museos*, Vol. LVII, 1951

Cardona, Maria de. 'El Palacio Orfei en Venecia y su donante' in *Semana*, 2 Feb 1954

Carlo, Achille de. *L'Arte a Venezia*. Padua, 1899

Chiappini di Sorio, Ileana. 'Velvets from Venice' in *Apollo*, Sept 1975

Conti, Angelo. *La Beata Riva, trattato dell'oblio*. Milan, 1900

Cooper, Diana. *The Rainbow comes and goes*. London, 1958

Cortes-Cavanillas, Julian. 'Recuerde España a Mariano Fortuny y Madrazo' in *ABC*, 11 Oct 1957

Cossart, Michael de. *The food of love: Princesse Edmond de Polignac and her Salon*. Hamish Hamilton, London, 1978

Damerini, Gino. 'D'Annunzio a Venezia' in *Quaderni D'Annunziani*, Vol. V, 1943

Damerini, Gino. 'Ricordi su Eleonora Duse e Gabriele D'Annunzio' in *Quaderni D'Annunziani*, Vols. XII–XIII, 1958

D'Annunzio, Gabriele. *Forse che si forse' che no*. Rome, 1932

Deschodt, Anne Marie. 'Seeking your Fortuny' in *The Sunday Times Magazine*, 23 July 1978

Deschodt, Anne Marie. *Mariano Fortuny: Un magicien de Venise*. Editions Du Regard, Paris, 1979

Dorner, Jane. *Fashion: the changing shape of fashion through the years*. Octopus Books, London, 1974

Duncan, Irma and Ross MacDougall, Allan. *Isadora Duncan*. London, 1919

Fallaci, Oriana. 'Un Leonardo spagnolo all'ombra di S. Marco' in *Epoca*, 1 Nov 1952

Fanelli, Giovanni e Rosalia. *Il disegno moderno: disegno, moda, architettura, 1890–1940*. Florence, 1976

Feder. 'Gli scenari del Tristano e Isotta alla Scala' in *La Lettura*, Vol. 1, Jan 1901

Fortuny y Madrazo, Mariano. *Éclairage Scénique: Systeme Fortuny*. Paris, 1904

Fortuny y Madrazo, Mariano (ed.). *Fortuny 1838–1874*. Bologna, 1933

Gallego, Julian. 'Marcel Proust, seleccion de ideas sobre el arte' in *Revista de Ideas Esteticas*, No. 13, July–Sept 1976

Gallego, Julian. 'Proust y Espana'. (To be published in *Revista de Occidente*.)

Garland, M. et al. *Fashion 1900–1939.* (A Scottish Arts Council Exhibition.) Idea Books, London, 1975

Gatti, Carlo. *Il teatro alla Scala nella storia e nell'arte (1778–1963).* Milan, 1964

Gish, Lilian and Pinchot, Ann. *Lilian Gish, the movies, Mr. Griffith and me.* New Jersey, 1969

Glynn, Prudence and Ginsburg, Madeleine. *In fashion: dress in the twentieth century.* George Allen and Unwin, London, 1978

Haddon, Celia. 'Enduring Fashion' in *The Sunday Times Magazine*, 1 March 1976

Hafemann, Ruth. *Die Darstellung des modischen Kostüms als literarisches Ausdrucksmittel bei Marcel Proust,* Berlin, 1935

Hahn, Reynaldo. *Notes: Journal d'un musicien.* Paris, 1933

Hale, Sheila. 'Fragments from the Fortuny Rainbow' in the *Daily Telegraph Magazine*, 27 Oct 1972

Henriot, Emile. 'Deshabillés' in *Gazette du Bon Ton*, Vol. I, Dec 1912

Holme, Charles (ed.). 'Modern etching and engraving, European and American' in the *Studio*, Special Summer Number, 1902

Howell, Georgina. *In Vogue: six decades of fashion.* Penguin, London, 1975

Huas, Jeanine. *Les femmes chez Proust.* Hachette, Paris, 1971

Jullian, Philippe. *D'Annunzio.* Pall Mall, London, 1972

Kindermann, Heinz. *Theathergeschichte Europas.* Salzburg, 1968

Lafuente Ferrari, Enrique. *La Vida y el arte de Ignacio Zuloaga.* Madrid, 1950

Lambert, Eleanor (ed.). *World of Fashion.* Bowker, Epping, Essex, 1976

Locatelli Milesi, Achille. 'Vecchi costumi in moderni ritratti femminili' in *Emporium*, No. 264, Dec 1916

Malaguzzi Valeri, Francesco. 'Le stoffe Fortuny' in *Cronache d'Arte*, Vol. IV, 1925

Marangoni, Guido, 'Le stoffe stampate della Società Anonima Fortuny' in *Le Arti Decorative*, April–May 1924

Marangoni, Guido. 'Le stoffe d'arte et l'arredamento della casa' in *Enciclopedia delle moderne arti decorative italiane,* Vol. V. Milan, 1928

Mariacher, G. *I vetri della raccolta Fortuny al museo di Murano.* Venice, 1959

Mariutti de Sanchez Rivero, Angela. *Quattro spagnoli a Venezia.* Venice, 1957

Marotti, Ferruccio. *Amleto o dell'oxymoron.* Rome, 1966

Minola de Gallotti, Mariana. 'El museo Fortuny de Venecia' in *Goya*, No. 128 Sept–Oct 1975

McCarthy, Mary. *The Group.* New York, 1963

Ojetti, Ugo. 'Fortuny' in *L'illustrazione italiana*, 27 Feb 1921

Ojetti, Ugo. *Cose Viste.* Milan, 1925

Omero Gallo, Giannino. 'La casa magica di S. Benedetto' in *L'Ambrosiano*, 1935

Omero Gallo, Giannino. 'La casa magica di Mariano Fortuny' in *Il Gazzettino*, 26 Aug 1935

Omero Gallo, Giannino. 'Luci della vita interiore, lettere di G. D'Annunzio a M. Fortuny y Madrazo' in *Il Roma della Domenica*, 10 Jan 1937

P.* V.* 'Gli scenari del Tristano ed Isotta' in *Emporium*, No. 73, Jan 1901

Painter, George D. *Marcel Proust: a Biography.* 2 vols. London, 1959 and 1965

Perocco, Guido, 'Mariano Fortuny visto una volta non si dimenticava più' in *Gazzetta di Venezia*, 26, 27 March 1957

Pica, Vittorio. 'L'arte mondiale alla III Esposizione di Venezia nel 1899' in *Emporium*, Special Issue, 1899

Pica, Vittorio. 'La Pittura all' esposizione di Parigi (1900)' in *Emporium*, No. 76, April 1901

Pica, V. and Del Massa, A. *Atlas de la Gravure Moderne.* Florence, 1928

Piot, René. *Les 'Tempere' Venitiennes de Mariano Fortuny.* Venice, 1933

Poppenberg, Felix, 'Dekorative variationen' in *Der Türmer*, Vol. I, 1907–8

Proust, Marcel. *A la Recherche du Temps Perdu*, ed. Pierre Clarac and André Ferré. 3 vols. Paris, 1954

Quennell, J. M. 'Precious Stuff: Fortuny' in *Vogue* (London), No. 15, Dec 1972

Quennell, J. M. 'Proust and Fashion' in *Marcel Proust (1871–1922): a Centenary Volume*, ed. Peter Quennell. Weidenfeld & Nicholson, London, 1971

Régnier, Henri de. *L'Altana ou la Vie Venitienne, 1899–1924.* 2 vols. Paris, 1927

Rouché, Jacques. *L'Art Theatral Moderne.* Paris, 1910.

Sansom, William. *Proust and his World.* Thames & Hudson, London, 1973

Sheppard, Eugenia. 'The Fortuny Dress', New York *Herald Tribune*, 12 Sept 1962

Spaini, Alberto. 'Fortuny' in *L'Italia Letteraria*, 29 July 1929

Spencer, Charles. *Leon Bakst.* Academy Editions, London, 1978

Stevenson, Sara and Bennet, Helen. *Van Dyck in Check Trousers: Fancy Dress in Art and Life, 1700–1900.* Trustees of the National Galleries of Scotland, 1978

Temple, Alfred George. *Modern Spanish Painting*. London, 1908

Toomey, Philippa. 'Fragments from the Life of a Master Designer' in *The Times*, 23 Dec 1974

Tumiati, Corrado. 'Il mio vicino mago' in *Corriere della Sera*, 6 Sept 1932

Whitney, Belle Armstrong. *What to Wear: A Book for Women*. Battle Creek, Michigan, 1916

Widor, Ch-M. 'Nouveau Système d'Eclairage de la Scene' in *Le Menestrel*, 15 April 1906

Zannier, Italo. 'Mariano Fortuny' in *Fotografia Italiana*, No. 2, 1977

EXHIBITION CATALOGUES

Granada, Universidad de Granada, Colegio Mayor S. Jeronimo. *Exposicion antologica de la Calcografia Nacional*. Sept–Oct 1975

London, Corporation of Art Gallery. *Works by Spanish Masters*. 1901

London, Wildenstein Gallery. *Marcel Proust and his Time (1871–1922)*. 1955

London, Victoria and Albert Museum. *Fashion: An Anthology by Cecil Beaton*. Oct 1971–Jan 1972 (Catalogue by Madeleine Ginsburg; Introduction by Cecil Beaton)

London, Victoria and Albert Museum. *Liberty's 1875–1975*. 1975

Los Angeles, Los Angeles County Museum; San Francisco, M. H. de Young Memorial Museum. *A Remembrance of Mariano Fortuny*. 1967–1968

Lyon, Musée Historique des Tissus; Brighton, Brighton Museum. *Mariano Fortuny (1871–1949)*. 1980 (Catalogue by Guillermo de Osma *et al.*)

Madrid, Biblioteca Nacional. *Exposicion Fortuny y Marsal y Fortuny y Madrazo*. June 1951 (Catalogue by Elena Paez)

Madrid, Biblioteca Nacional. *Antologia del Grabado espagnol*. Oct 1952 (Catalogue by Elena Paez)

Madrid, Fundacion Juan March. *Exposicion antologica de la Calcografia Nacional*.

Oct–Nov 1975 (Catalogue by Antonio Gallego *et al.*)

Milan, Galeria Dedalo. *Mariano Fortuny y Madrazo*. Nov 1935 (Introduction by M. Zamacois)

New York, Brooklyn Museum. *Changing Fashion, 1800–1970*. 1972 (Catalogue by Elizabeth Ann Coleman)

New York, Fashion Institute of Technology. *Paul Poiret*. 25 May–11 Sept 1976

New York, Metropolitan Museum of Art. *Vanity Fair*. 1977–8

Paris, *Exposition Internationale de 1900*. General catalogue
—Catalogo de los expositores de España (Madrid 1900)

Paris, *Exposition Internationale des Arts Decoratifs et Industriels Modernes. 1925*. Rapport General Illustré
—Catalogue General Officiel
—L'Italie, Catalogue Illustré
—Rapport General, Vol VI: Tissu et Papier (classes 13 and 14)
—Rapport General, Vol X: Theatre, Photographie et Cinematographie (classes 25 and 37)

Paris, Galerie Hector Brame. *Mariano Fortuny y Madrazo*. March 1934 (Introduction by M. Zamacois)

Paris, Musée du Costume de la Ville de Paris. *Elegantes Parisiennes au temps de M.*

Proust, 1890–1916. Dec 1968–April 1969

Paris, Musée du Costume de la Ville de Paris. *Vingt ans après, principaux enrichissements, 1956–76*. Dec 1978–April 1979

Paris, Musée Jacquemart-André. *Marcel Proust et son temps*. 1971 (Preface by J. Cain)

Paris, Musée de la Mode et du Costume. *Secrets d'elégance*. Dec 1978–April 1980

Paris, Societé Nationale des Beaux Arts. *Catalogue illustré du Salon de 1899, de Salon de 1900* et *du Salon de 1902*

Venice, Ca Pesaro (Museo d'Arte Moderna), *Incisioni di M. Fortuny y Marsal e di M. Fortuny y Madrazo*. April 1965

Venice. *Esposizione Internationale d'Arte* (later *Biennale Internationale d'Arte*). Catalogues for 1895, 1899, 1922, 1924, 1928, 1930, 1934, 1936, 1950

Venice, *XIX Exposizione Biennale Internationale d'Arte*. Catalogo della Mostra Espagnola. 1934

Venice, *XXV Exposición Bienal de arte en Venecia*. Catalogo del pabellón espanol. 1950

Venice, Biennale di Venezia. *Eleonora Duse*. 23 Sept–13 Oct 1969

Venice, Palazzo Fortuny. *Immagini e materiali del laboratorio Fortuny*. 1978 (Catalogue by Fuso, Mescola and Zannier)

Index